G. M.
11/93

DATE DUE

MY 21 '93			
JE 18 '93			
RENEW			
AP 29 '94			
AP 17 '95			
SE 22 '95			
MY 17 '96			
OC 31 '96			

DEMCO 38-296

HAND, REEF
and STEER

Also by Richard Henderson

Better Sailing
Sailing in Windy Weather
Singlehanded Sailing
Sailing at Night
Understanding Rigs and Rigging
Heavy Weather Guide (with William J. Kotsch)
John G. Alden and His Yacht Designs (with Robert Carrick)
Fifty-three Boats You Can Build
The Racing-Cruiser
Sail and Power
Philip L. Rhodes and His Yacht Designs
Choice Yacht Designs

HAND, REEF and STEER

A Practical Handbook on Sailing

Written and Illustrated by
Richard Henderson

CB
CONTEMPORARY
BOOKS

CHICAGO

Library of Congress Cataloging-in-Publication Data

Henderson, Richard 1924–
    Hand, reef and steer : a practical handbook on sailing / written
and illustrated by Richard Henderson.
       p.   cm.
    Includes index.
    ISBN 0-8092-4010-6 (pbk.) : $11.95
    1. Sailing—Handbooks, manuals, etc.   I. Title.
GV811.H362   1991
797.1′24—dc20   90-25587
                                              CIP

Published by Contemporary Books, Inc.
180 North Michigan Avenue, Chicago, Illinois 60601
Manufactured in the United States of America
International Standard Book Number: 0-8092-4010-6

In memory of
C. LOWNDES JOHNSON

CONTENTS

LIST OF ILLUSTRATIONS

AUTHOR'S PREFACE

Although there are excellent books on sailing in print, many are far too technical for the beginner. Other books designed specifically for the novice lack detail in boat handling, sail trim, and particularly in helmsmanship. This book attempts to stress these subjects in the simplest way and present basic principles of sailing. Without a grounding in these principles no beginner should attempt to sail alone. Once he has mastered the essentials, he will be ready to enjoy one of the most rewarding of all sports—sailing a boat. Sailing builds self-reliance, patience, humility, sportsmanship, and respect for others in all of us. I know of no better training ground for young people.

The expression "hand, reef, and steer" goes back to the days of square-rigged sailing ships. It referred to the principal skills required of an able-bodied seaman. Today, the expression is often used in a very broad sense to imply general proficiency as a sailor.

I would like to thank C. Lowndes Johnson of Easton, Maryland, for looking over the original manuscript and for his valuable comments and encouragement; Victor Jorgensen of *The Skipper* magazine for advice on changes in "The Rules of the Road"; Edmund Henderson of the University of Delaware for literary and technical advice; and Veronica Amoss of the Naval Institute for editorial information. My very special thanks and appreciation go to Jean Kellogg, who is primarily responsible for the book's existence.

HAND, REEF and STEER

A schooner, yawl, or cutter in charge of a capable man seems to handle herself as if endowed with the power of reasoning and the gift of swift execution. One laughs with sheer pleasure at a smart piece of maneuvering, as at a manifestation of a living creature's quick wit and graceful precision.

Joseph Conrad, *Mirror of the Sea*

TERMS

AN INTRODUCTION TO NAUTICAL TERMS

The science of sailing has a special nomenclature which the novice should learn well. This section will deal with a few basic terms he should memorize before he attempts to proceed. More nautical words will be introduced later. The following procedure will be used throughout the book: The first time a nautical term is used, it will be italicized. If it is not explained in the text or diagram, it will be marked by an asterisk and will be explained at the bottom of the page. In addition, these terms will appear in the index at the back of the book. The simplest and most untechnical explanations have been used throughout.

Figure 1 deals mostly with directional nomenclature. It shows the outline of a boat as if we were looking down on her. (Incidentally, boats and ships are always referred to in the feminine gender.) The *bow* is the front or the *fore* part of a boat, while the *stern* is the back or *after* part. When facing the bow while on a boat, we look *forward*. When facing the stern, we look *aft*. When one object on the boat is closer to the stern than a second object, we say it is *abaft* the second. The *starboard* side of a boat is the right-hand side when looking forward, and the *port* side is on the left. Here is an easy way to remember this. A FORWARD LOOKING MAN HAS RED PORT (WINE) LEFT. In the expression, "red" refers to the color of the port side running light when a vessel is *under way* or moving. A green light is carried on the starboard side.

Amidships is the middle of a boat either midway between the sides or the bow and stern. *Inboard* means toward amidships, while *outboard* means toward or beyond a boat's side or end. *Aboard* is being on a boat, while *overboard* is not. *Abeam* refers to an object's *bearing* (or its direction) off the side when it is at right angles to the direction in which the boat is headed.

Sailors have a system for indicating directions which consists of dividing the entire distance around a boat into 32 points. From *dead ahead*, or directly in front of the bow, to the beam, or that point from which an object bears abeam, is 8 points. From the beam to the stern would be 8 more points, making a total of 16 points from bow to stern or a total of 32 points all the way around. An object bearing on the *quarter* bears anywhere from *dead astern*, or directly aft, to *broad on the quarter*, or 4 points abaft the beam.

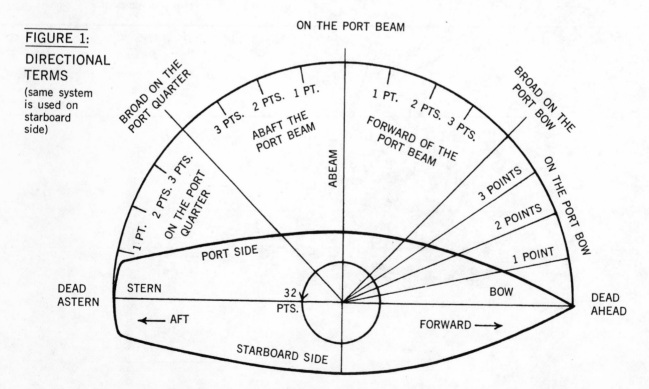

FIGURE 1:

DIRECTIONAL TERMS

(same system is used on starboard side)

ON THE PORT BEAM

BROAD ON THE PORT QUARTER

3 PTS. 2 PTS. 1 PT.

ABAFT THE PORT BEAM

1 PT. 2 PTS. 3 PTS.

FORWARD OF THE PORT BEAM

BROAD ON THE PORT BOW

ABEAM

1 PT. 2 PTS. 3 PTS.

ON THE PORT QUARTER

ON THE PORT BOW

3 POINTS

2 POINTS

1 POINT

PORT SIDE

DEAD ASTERN

STERN

32 PTS.

BOW

DEAD AHEAD

← AFT

FORWARD →

STARBOARD SIDE

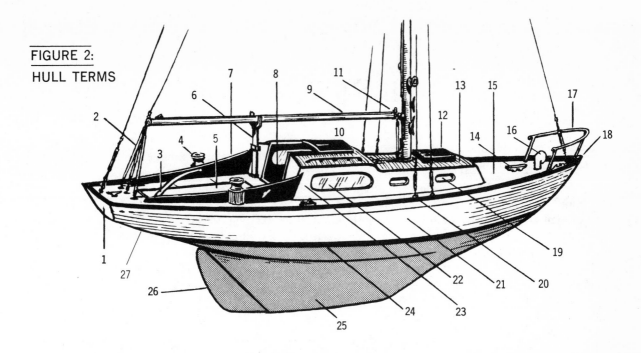

FIGURE 2:
HULL TERMS

1 TRANSOM	10 COMPANIONWAY SLIDE	19 PORTHOLE
2 MAIN SHEET	11 GOOSENECK	20 CHAIN-PLATE
3 TILLER	12 FORWARD HATCH COVER	21 TOPSIDES
4 WINCH	13 CABIN TOP	22 DOGHOUSE LIGHT (WINDOW)
5 COCKPIT	14 BOW CLEAT	23 DOGHOUSE
6 BOOM CRUTCH	15 FORE DECK	24 BOOT TOP
7 COCKPIT COAMING	16 VENTILATOR	25 KEEL
8 COMPANIONWAY	17 BOW PULPIT	26 RUDDER
9 MAIN BOOM	18 STEM HEAD	27 COUNTER

Figure 2 shows some of the principal parts of a vessel. Terms dealing with boat construction and shape will be brought up in Section III.

The boat shown in Figure 2 is a typical small cabin sailer. A *cabin* is the roofed-over shelter that usually has some accommodations for living aboard with a *galley* (kitchen) and *bunks* (beds). When one enters a cabin, he goes *below*, not downstairs. He goes down the *companionway*, which is a stairway leading into the cabin. That part of the cabin which sticks up above the *hull*, or main body of the boat, is called the *cabin house*. Windows in the cabin house are called *portholes* or port-lights.

The flat after surface of a square-sterned hull is the *transom*. Beneath the transom, slightly farther forward, is the *counter*. At the top edge of the hull is the *rail*, and slightly under that is the *deck*, which is the planked-over, horizontal surface we walk on. In open boats (without decks), we usually call a hull's top edge the *gunwale* (pronounced gun'l). Openings cut through the deck or cabin house which may be closed by covers are *hatches*.

The *cockpit* is a large sunken or open area in the deck where people sit. The *helmsman*, one who steers, usually sits in the cockpit where he can reach the *tiller*, which is a sort of steering handle. The tiller is connected to the *rudder*, a vertical, movable plate abaft the keel*. The rudder moves underwater on hinges called *gudgeons* and *pintles* so that it may turn the boat. Cockpits nearly always have built-up sides around them to prevent water from washing in. These are called *cockpit coamings*.

A horizontal pole called the *boom* is attached to the mast by a sort of hinge called a *gooseneck*. When the boat is not under sail, her boom usually rests in a *boom crutch*. The mast is held up by *stays* or *standing rigging*.

Figure 2 represents only a simple starting point for the beginner in learning a boat's nomenclature. Terms for rigging and sails will be described in some detail in Sections IV and V.

---

*Keel—A boat's constructional backbone at her bottom running fore and aft. It is often extended downward deeply (as in Fig. 2) to supply lateral resistance. (Also see Figs. 5 and 7.)

FIRST BOAT

PURPOSE OF THE BOAT

The correct choice of a boat is tremendously important to the beginning sailor. At the very outset he should determine for what purpose the boat will be used. Most boats are designed for some primary purpose or for the best possible performance under particular conditions. Some boats are designed for class racing, others for family daysailing, others for cruising. Some racers are designed to perform best while going to *windward*** in a choppy sea, others for high-speed planing in relatively smooth water. Some cruisers are designed primarily for comfort and ease of handling, while with others the accent is on seaworthiness. The boat designer must usually accentuate one quality at the expense of another.

To determine properly the purpose of his boat, the prospective owner should ask himself the following questions: Where will the boat be used? Are the waters protected? Are the winds light or heavy—gusty or steady? Are the waters deep or shallow? What are the facilities at the yacht club or home port? How many and what kind of boats are there? Will he eventually use the boat to cruise in? Might he eventually wish to race? Will he be sailing by himself most of the time, or will he be taking out his family or friends? Will he take children? How much time has he to spend on the boat?

All these questions must be carefully considered in addition to the obvious one—what kind of boat can he afford to buy and maintain?

SIZE AND BASIC REQUIREMENTS

Many people believe that a beginner's first boat should be a small one, but I do not necessarily agree. Although small boats are usually more responsive, one can learn just as well in a smart sailing medium-sized boat, or even a fairly large boat. Small boats are fine for youngsters, but most adults do not like to be crammed into a cockleshell; furthermore most would wish, on occasion at least, to take out friends or family. Also, while there are many desirable small sailboats, some are tricky to handle and easy to *capsize**.

The most essential requirements of a first boat, regardless of size, are sound design and smart sailing ability. This means that a boat must have the proper balance, stability, and responsiveness to the *helm**. The beginner is seriously handicapped if he tries to learn in an old, heavy tub that is slow *in stays **, *yaws** excessively when *running before the wind**, or has an arm-wrenching *weather helm** in a breeze. The behavior and performance of a boat depend primarily on the shape of her hull and the plan of her rig. These will be discussed in the next two sections.

SAFETY FEATURES

There are a few safety features which every beginner's boat should have. If the boat is small, with a half deck and open cockpit, she should have an ample *washboard* (Figure 3, *A*) to keep *green water** out of the cockpit. She also should have reasonably high coamings, especially if the boat is a *centerboarder**. Should the boat capsize, her skipper, after righting her, will be better able to bail her out if the coamings are sufficiently high to keep waves from sloshing in. In addition, if the boat has decking, it should be wide enough from rail to cockpit to prevent waves from washing in when the boat is sailing heeled over in choppy waters. If the boat will not float when *swamped**, she should have air tanks or some kind of built-in flotation (see "Capsizing" in Section XIII).

A large boat with cabin should have a *self-bailing cockpit* as shown in Figure 3, *B*. This cockpit consists of a watertight cockpit-well with drains in its bottom which obviously must be higher than the surface of the water upon which the boat is floating so that any

---

Windward—Up wind or against the wind.
Capsize—To turn over so that the mast is in the water.

Helm—Tiller or wheel by which a boat is steered.
In stays—Extremely sluggish when turning through the wind (see Fig. 34).
Yaw—Sudden veering from side to side.
Running before the wind—With the wind from behind (see Fig. 19).
Weather helm—Tendency for a boat to head up into the wind (see Fig. 11).
Green water—A solid wave not merely foam.
Centerboarder—A boat with centerboard or movable board which supplies lateral resistance (see Fig. 5, *B*).
Swamped—To be filled with water.

FIGURE 3: SOME RECOMMENDED SAFETY FEATURES

A. FOR SMALL HALF-DECKED BOATS

B. FOR CABIN SAILERS
(see figure 96 for boat with motor)

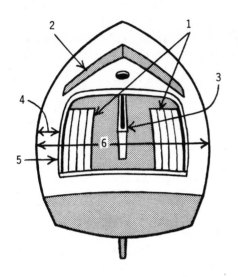

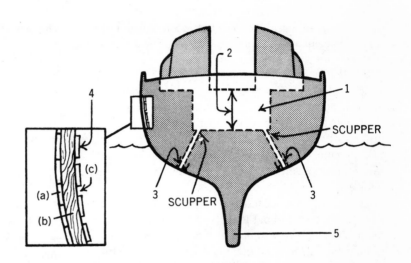

1 FLOTATION under cockpit seats and/or at bow and stern or in other locations so that boat floats level and fairly high when swamped (see fig. 94)

2 AMPLE WASHBOARD (often called splashboard)

3 HIGH CENTERBOARD WELL if it is open at the top (see fig. 94 for explanation)

4 SUFFICIENT SIDE DECK

5 AMPLE COCKPIT COAMINGS

6 AMPLE BEAM (WIDTH) FOR STABILITY (see section III)

1 SELF-BAILING COCKPIT (watertight cockpit well with scupper pipe drains)

2 COMPANIONWAY WITH BOTTOM RAISED FAR ABOVE COCKPIT'S BOTTOM (see figure 2) ALSO THERE SHOULD BE A FORWARD HATCH LARGE ENOUGH FOR ALTERNATE EXIT WITH LATCHING COVER.

3 SEACOCKS located where all below water pipes or hoses pass through hull

4 CEILING ON WOOD BOATS WITH SLOTS AND IN GENERAL NO DEAD AIR SPACES (to prevent rot) (a) planks (b) rib (c) space

5 AMPLE BALLAST (WEIGHT) ON KEEL FOR STABILITY (see section III)

accumulated water in the cockpit's bottom will run out. Aside from adding to the safety of a boat, this feature is a great convenience, for the owner can leave his boat at a mooring without setting a canvas cockpit cover to keep out rainwater.

In the opinion of many experienced sailors, every boat with any outlet or intake opening through her hull should have *seacocks*, or marine-type shut-off valves, at the openings. These will occur at the *head**, sink, cockpit *scuppers**, and water intake for the engine, if there is one. Seacocks can keep a boat from sinking in the event of a broken or leaking pipe or hose.

Although this book deals entirely with sailboats, no discussion of safety features would be complete without mention of the danger from gasoline fumes. Many boating accidents are caused by gas explosions and fires. If a boat has an inboard engine, and many sailboats have *auxiliaries**, her engine compartment needs more than adequate ventilation. She should also have a *blower* or powered air exhaust system which will reach the deepest part of the *bilge**, because fumes tend to settle there.

Auxiliaries—Secondary propulsion power in the form of a small engine in sailboats.
Bilge—A boat's bottom between her keel and sides. Also the lower area inside the hull under the floor boards, where water often accumulates.

Head—Marine W.C.
Scuppers—Drains (see Fig. 3, B).

MATERIALS

Boats can be made of a variety of materials. Many of these materials are relatively new, such as marine plywood, fiberglass, and aluminum. These all have advantages and disadvantages; however, in most cases the advantages outweigh the disadvantages.

Plywood is most often seen in small boats. It has tremendous strength and is usually economical; but it must be adequately painted to prevent surface checks, and its ends should be thoroughly covered to prevent water from seeping in between the plies.

Fiberglass has become a popular material. It has great strength and resistance to deterioration, but the prospective buyer of a plastic boat should not be lulled by advertisements into thinking it will be completely maintenance-free from year to year. All too frequently there are problems with blisters below the waterline, and eventually the topsides will need painting after they become faded or scratched. Furthermore, the bottom, as with every boat that floats in salt water, must be painted with an *antifouling** paint. A fiberglass boat should have adequate *bulkheads** and other structural members because of the flexible nature of this material. Without sufficient hull support, a plastic boat might be unable to carry her rigging *taut**.

Aluminum is not only light in weight, but it also has great structural strength and rigidity. It cannot be pulled out of shape. Deterioration of the newest aluminum alloys is extremely slow; however, there is a danger of galvanic corrosion in salt water. This can be prevented by eliminating the direct contact of dissimilar metals by adequate insulation and the use of prime coats under metal-base paints. Aluminum hulls can be expensive, and they are apt to be somewhat noisy.

While wood may require more maintenance than certain other materials, it is hard to beat in appearance. The main form of deterioration in a wood hull is rot, but this can be largely prevented if the boat is properly ventilated. There should be a free circulation of air in every nook and cranny, particularly in those places where rainwater might accumulate. I am in favor of slots in the *ceilings** (see Figure 3, *B*) and anywhere else where there may be a dead space. Wood boats enjoy a long life when they are properly built and cared for. It is not uncommon to see a wood boat out sailing that is over 40 years old.

SURVEY

The soundest advice anyone can give a prospective used-boat buyer is to have any vessel thoroughly surveyed before purchasing her. There are professional surveyors who specialize in examining boats for constructional defects and deterioration. Such examinations before sale are a wise and customary practice. The surveyor knows where and how to look for rot and corrosion, and he will point out any dangerous conditions or areas of potential trouble. It is customary for the prospective buyer to pay for the *hauling** and survey, but these are expenses that are well worthwhile, for they can ensure a wise purchase.

---

*Antifouling—Discouraging to barnacles, worms, and marine growth.
*Bulkheads—Upright partitions (see Fig. 8).
*Taut—Tight.

*Ceiling—Inner skin or planking inside the ribs.
*Hauling—A boat being pulled out of water.

THE HULL

DESCRIPTIVE TERMS

In order to understand the basic behavior of boats, the beginning sailor should acquire a little knowledge of the shape or form of a hull. A few simple terms used to describe these shapes are illustrated in Figure 4.

The *load waterline* (L.W.L.) is a horizontal line around a boat where the surface of the water meets the hull. A boat's *draft* is the vertical distance from the L.W.L. to the deepest part of the boat. *Deadrise* is the rise or the upward slant of a boat's bottom measured vertically. A flat-bottomed boat has no deadrise. *Entrance* is the sharpening of a boat's bow where it enters the water. It can be hollow or full. A boat's *run* is her underwater bottom near the stern. *Forefoot* refers to the depth of a hull underwater near the bow below her entrance. A boat's *beam* is her width from side to side at the widest point. *Freeboard* is the vertical distance from the load waterline to the rail. *Overhang* occurs at the bow and stern. It accounts for the difference between a boat's length on the waterline and her maximum length or *length overall*. *Sheer* is the horizontal curve along the rail or deck from bow to stern. *Flare* is an outward slant of the sides usually near the bows, while *tumble home* is an inward curve of the upper sides which usually occurs amidships and at the stern.

FIGURE 4: DESCRIPTIVE TERMS FOR THE HULL

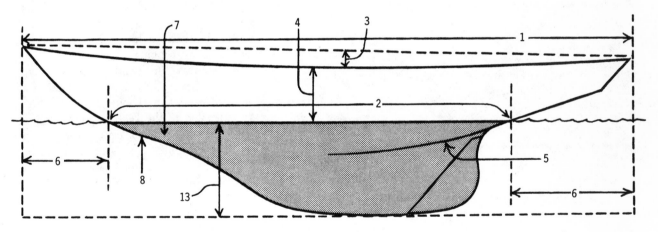

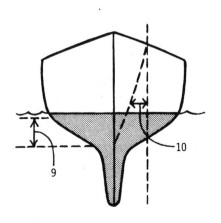

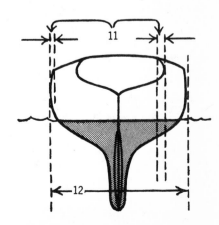

1 LENGTH OVERALL
2 LOAD WATERLINE
3 SHEER
4 FREEBOARD
5 RUN
6 OVERHANGS
7 ENTRANCE
8 FOREFOOT
9 DEADRISE
10 FLARE
11 TUMBLE HOME
12 BEAM
13 DRAFT

LEE-BOARDS

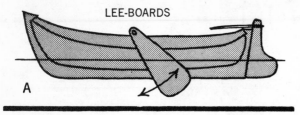

A

CENTERBOARD

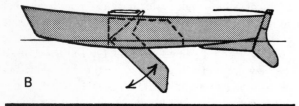

B

DAGGERBOARD

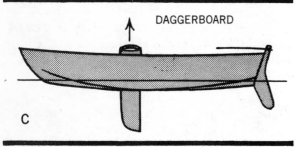

C

FULL-LENGTH DEEP KEEL

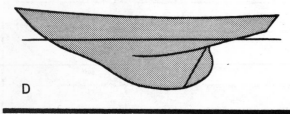

D

FIN KEEL

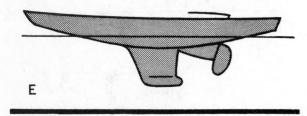

E

KEEL-CENTERBOARD

F

LATERAL RESISTANCE

Every sailboat's hull needs some form of lateral resistance under water; otherwise the boat would, on certain points of sailing, be blown sideways by the wind or *make leeway*. Figure 5 shows the various methods of overcoming leeway.

A shows a boat with *lee-boards*, which are fastened to each side and can be pivoted so as to swing up or down. They are used with great success on some foreign boats, particularly in Holland, where many boats are designed to sit on the bottom because of shallow water and extreme tides. In this country, lee-boards are not generally considered the most practical form of lateral resistance on large craft. Here they are most often used on small sailing canoes.

The boat in B is equipped with a *centerboard*, which is a board hinged at one end enabling the other end to be slid up or down into a narrow box or *well* in the boat's center. The centerboard may be raised when on certain points of sailing in shoal waters. This is a particularly handy arrangement for small boats which must be pulled out of water onto a ramp or beach.

The *daggerboard*, shown in C, is a kind of centerboard except that it is not hinged but slides all the way out of its well. This arrangement has two disadvantages not shared by the centerboard. First, in not being hinged, the daggerboard will not absorb as much shock if the boat should run aground; and, second, when the board is up, its top sticks up high and presents an obstruction to the boom swinging across.

Illustration D shows a full-length *deep-keel* boat. Technically speaking, every boat has some kind of a keel—it is the constructional backbone of a boat; but in D, we see an extension of the keel to supply lateral resistance. Most deep-keel boats have a metal weight at the keel's bottom for stability. This weight should be sufficient to prevent the boat from capsizing under almost any normal sailing condition. Another advantage of the deep keel is that it saves room in the cockpit or cabin by eliminating the centerboard well. An obvious disadvantage is that the deep-keel boat cannot go into extremely shallow waters. It is also more difficult to get off the bottom after a grounding. Another slight disadvantage of the deep keel is that it cannot be adjusted like a board to get additional speed on certain points of sailing.

The *fin keel*, shown in E, has practically the same advantages and disadvantages of the full-length deep keel except that it is not generally considered to be quite as seaworthy; however, because of its thinness and less wetted area, it usually offers less forward resistance, making the hull slightly faster. Unlike the deep keel, which is an integral part of a boat's bottom, the fin is often a separate, flat plate, usually made of iron or lead, which is bolted to a boat's bottom. Fins are used on many small racing classes such as International 110s and Stars.

Weighted keels are generally recommended for areas where the waters are fairly deep and where the breezes can get fresh. They are obviously advantageous on any boat with a cabin because there is usually a lot of bedding and other gear in a cabin that would be ruined or at least harmed by a soaking should the boat capsize. Of course, a cabin centerboarder is reasonably safe from capsizing if she has enough beam and *inside ballast**. Some boats, usually large ones, have a combination of centerboard and keel (Figure 5, *F*). A short centerboard slides up into a relatively shallow weighted keel. Then the boat sacrifices no room in her cabin and will be almost as uncapsizable as a deep-keel boat.

HULL FORM

Sailing hulls come in a variety of forms. They can be flat, round, V-shaped, or some combination of these (see Figure 6). The style you choose will depend upon where and what kind of sailing you intend to do. A shallow, almost flat V, or round bottom is used on a *planing* hull, which gains tremendous speed by lifting up and riding on its bow wave. The flatter bottom having little deadrise enables a light displacement boat to skim over the water's surface rather than plow through it. Cruising boats and family daysailers, which are not intended to be quite as sporty, have deeper bottoms with more deadrise to give an easier motion and lessen pounding when driving into a head sea. Wood hulls with V-bottoms are generally considered easier and more economical to construct than those with round bottoms. But the round form tends to pound less in head seas, and when conventionally built of wood, it is considered by most authorities to be stronger (for given frame and planking size) because of resistance to bending and the fact that outside water pressure actually forces the planks together.

Looking at a boat's hull from her side, we can consider her profile: her sheer, overhangs, forefoot, and draft. Sheer is largely an aesthetic matter. Some boats have a pronounced sheer, others are straight, and a few have the *reverse sheer* or humpbacked look. The usual purpose of sheer is to have a boat's ends high enough so that seas will not break over her bow or over her stern when they are following. I prefer the look of a moderate sheer, but that is mostly a matter of personal taste.

Many racing boats, particularly those of the narrow, deep-hull form, such as Meter boats (Figure 7, *B*), have

Inside ballast—Pigs of lead or similar weights secured under the floorboards in the bilge.

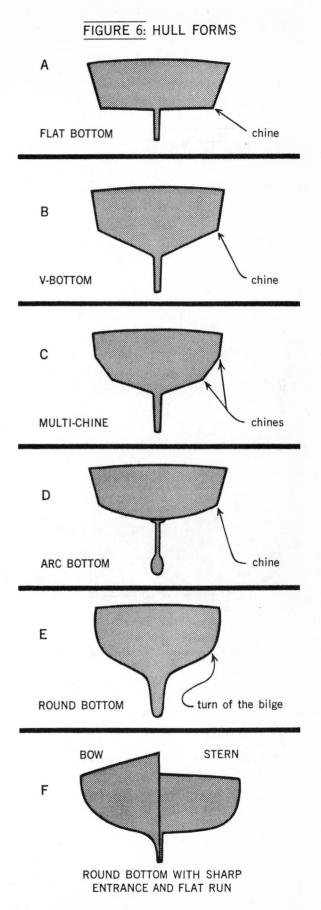

FIGURE 6: HULL FORMS

A — FLAT BOTTOM — chine

B — V-BOTTOM — chine

C — MULTI-CHINE — chines

D — ARC BOTTOM — chine

E — ROUND BOTTOM — turn of the bilge

F — BOW — STERN — ROUND BOTTOM WITH SHARP ENTRANCE AND FLAT RUN

FIGURE 7: HULL TYPES

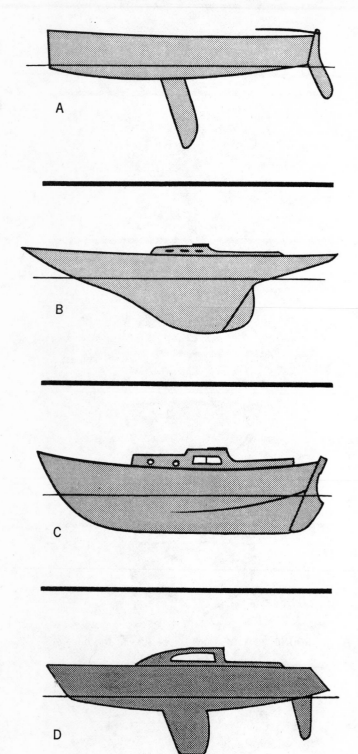

long overhangs. The main purpose of these overhangs is to increase a boat's waterline length as she heels over, thereby increasing her theoretical speed potential. The further the boat heels, the more her ends are submerged, and the maximum speed of a displacement or nonplaning hull depends upon her waterline length. A hull's top speed through the water expressed in *knots* or nautical miles per hour is about 1.34 times the square root of her waterline length. Sea boats and cruising boats tend to have fairly short ends mainly to lessen pounding in a seaway. Many small planing boats have short overhangs because they are usually designed to get their speed from sailing upright, the best position for planing; therefore they would benefit little from long overhangs.

High freeboard keeps a boat dry when in rough waters. This is obviously desirable, but the height of freeboard is sometimes so overdone that it detracts from a boat's appearance.

Cut-away forefoots are common on most racing boats. This enables the boat to turn quickly, but she will yaw in following seas. On the other hand, sea boats tend to have deeper forefoots so that they can be steered easily in a following sea, but this makes them slow to turn.

Figure 7 illustrates in four different types of boats the variations in sheer, overhangs, and forefoot. Figure 7, A shows a small, light, planing daysailer or racer with very little deadrise. She has practically no overhangs and a straight sheer. Figure 7, B is a Meter boat, racing type, with long overhangs, cut-away forefoot, and moderate sheer. Figure 7, C is an offshore cruiser with short overhangs, deep forefoot, and pronounced sheer. And Figure 7, D is a modern cruising-racer with very little sheer and overhangs, a reverse transom, a deep fin keel, and a spade rudder well separated from the keel.

In making the correct choice of hull form, the beginning sailor should match his hull to the main purpose for which the boat is intended. No matter what the choice, it is always the safest policy to buy a proven class boat or one designed by a recognized naval architect.

STABILITY AND ANGLE OF HEEL

Everyone knows the wind's lateral force against a sail causes a boat to *heel*, or lean to one side. A sailboat must have sufficient stability or resistance to this heeling force to carry adequate sail in a good breeze. Proper stability also becomes a safety factor in helping to prevent the capsizing or even the sinking of a heavily ballasted boat lacking flotation. There are two principal factors in a hull's design which affect its stability: beam and ballast. Centerboard boats depend primarily on wide beam for their stability, while keel boats depend on their ballasted keels. The deeper the keel, the lower the boat's center of gravity and hence the greater her stability. Obviously, the weight of the ballast affects the stability also. An average keel boat with moderate beam and sail area carries about one-third or more of her weight in ballast at the bottom of her keel. A deep-sea cruising boat is generally designed to have a great deal of reserve stability, but less *initial stability* than a racing boat. High initial stability, occurring during the first few degrees of heel, causes an unpleasant, jerky motion especially undesirable in a cruising boat; however, a racer is willing to tolerate some of this discomfort in order to carry more sail for greater speed. Boats which are *tender* (heel over too easily) may be made more stable by placing lead weights in the bilge, but great pains must be taken to see that this ballast is properly secured because otherwise it might shift when the boat receives a *knockdown* or severe heeling.

Most small centerboarders have no keel on which to carry ballast and they depend on human weight to remain upright in a breeze. Skipper and crew should *hike* or move their weight as far as possible to windward on the boat's high side. Often this is effectively accomplished with the use of *hiking straps* secured at the bottom of the cockpit and under which a sailor can hook his feet so that he can lean far out to windward. Sometimes a skipper use a *tiller extension*, a movable arm bolted to the end of the tiller, so that he may reach the tiller while hiking.

On most points of sailing the average boat sails best when heeled slightly to *leeward*, or toward the low side when the boat is heeled over. One reason for this is that in light air gravity causes the sails to sag to leeward and to assume a fuller shape. V-bottom boats should generally be sailed at greater angles of heel than those with round bottoms. Many boats with V-bottoms seem to go best on most points of sailing when their windward *chine*, the sharp angle where the side and the bottom join, is just kissing the water. Almost any boat with long overhangs—such as type B in Figure 7—will perform well when moderately heeled, because the heeling will increase the waterline length.

Most hulls, however, should not be heeled excessively. Even if a boat has a keel and cannot easily capsize, she will develop a bad weather helm partly because of her curved side being submerged and her bow being pushed to windward by her lee bow wave and also because thrust from the upper sail area is positioned to leeward, creating a turning moment around the hull's center of resistance. Helm balance will be discussed further in the section on heavy-weather sailing.

CONSTRUCTION

No discussion of the hull would be complete without showing at least a simple construction plan. In Figure 8, A and B illustrate the basic structural parts of a typical wood boat.

A boat is built with an internal supporting skeleton and an external skin. The main support in a skeleton is its backbone, which in a boat is a keel. Bolted to the keel at right angles or crosswise are the *floors*, or *floor timbers*, and growing up from these in the same direction are the *frames*, or *ribs*. The main support forward is the *stem*; while at the stern, in a square-sterned boat, it's the *horn timber* and transom. Along the ribs at the turn of the bilge, running fore and aft, is the *bilge stringer* or, on a sharp-bilged boat, it's the *chine log*. At the top of the ribs, running fore aft, are secured the *clamp* and *deck shelf*, which support the *deck beams*. These beams are horizontal structural members that run *athwartships* or across the ship, while *carlines* (or *carlins*) are the deck members that run fore and aft. *Mast partners* are heavy horizontal members supporting the mast at each side where it comes through the deck. The *heel* or bottom part of the mast is placed in a hollowed out block called the *mast step* which usually sits on the keel, although some small, modern boats have their masts stepped on their decks or cabin house tops. Cabin floorboards are often referred to as the *cabin sole*.

A boat's skin, as previously mentioned, can be composed of a variety of materials, but when it is wood-planked, there are two chief methods of construction used—clinker (shown in Figure 8, C) and carvel (Figure 8, D). In the clinkerbuilt boat, the planks, or *strakes* as they are often called, overlap like shingles on a roof; but in the carvel form of construction, the plank's edges are flush, making a smooth hull surface.

(See Figure 8 on the following page.)

FIGURE 8: HULL CONSTRUCTION

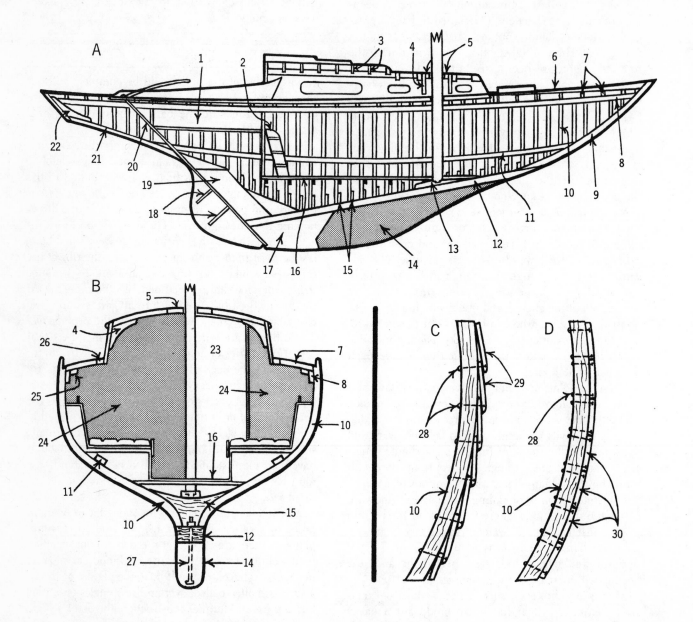

1 COCKPIT WELL	9 STEM	17 FALSE KEEL	25 DECK SHELF
2 COMPANION LADDER	10 RIB OR FRAME	18 RUDDER STRAPS	26 CARLINE OR CARLIN
3 CABIN BEAMS	11 BILGE STRINGER	19 DEADWOOD	27 KEEL BOLT
4 HANGING KNEE	12 KEEL	20 RUDDER STOCK	28 FASTENINGS
5 MAST PARTNERS	13 MAST STEP	21 HORN TIMBER	29 CLINKER PLANKS OR LAP-STRAKE
6 RAIL	14 BALLAST KEEL	22 STERN KNEE	30 CARVEL PLANKING
7 DECK BEAMS	15 FLOOR TIMBERS	23 DOORWAY	
8 CLAMP	16 CABIN SOLE	24 BULKHEAD	

THE RIG

KINDS OF RIGS

Now that we have examined a boat's hull, let us look at a boat's rig or mast and sail plan, which is the system used for harnessing the wind to propel the hull. Sailing rigs are divided into two general classes: the square rig and the fore and aft (see Figure 9). The square is undoubtedly the oldest rig, having in all probability been used on the first sailboat. It reached its highest degree of development in the days of the clippership. This rig is most efficient when the wind is abaft the beam or when a squarerigger has the wind behind her. The top of a squaresail is secured to a *yard*, which is a horizontal pole running athwartships that may be swung fore and aft to a limited extent by *lines** called *braces*. Except for an occasional squaresail or a deep-sea boat expected to sail before the trade winds, or on a training ship, one seldom sees this kind of sail today. Squareriggers have been outmoded by the *fore and aft rigged* boat, which can sail much closer to the wind. Before they began to fade from existence, squareriggers reached a high degree of rig variation and complexity, but since they are almost a thing of the past, we will deal only with rig variations in the fore and aft class.

The fore and aft sail is one which is usually pulled in by a line called a *sheet* and has its forward edge attached to a mast, stay, or semi-fixed location. It may be *trimmed** much closer or more nearly fore and aft than a squaresail. There are several basic types of sails in the fore and aft category: the *lateen, lug, sprit, gaff,* and *Marconi* (see Figure 9). The first two types are ancient. The lateen is said to have originated with the Arabs and is still popular in the general Mediterranean area. Lugs can still be seen in various parts of the world, particularly in China, where they have been used for centuries. The sprit rig is also an old if not ancient rig that was and still is used mostly on fishing boats, barges, and other *workboats**. In this country today, however, one rarely sees the sprit or lug except occasionally as a ship's lifeboat rig or on the sprit-rigged

Lines—General term for ropes on a boat.
Trimmed—Adjusted by a sheet.
Workboats—Commercial boats, not pleasure craft or yachts.

FIGURE 9: SAILING RIGS

SQUARE RIG

FORE AND AFT RIGS

LATEEN

SPRIT

LUG

GAFF

MARCONI

"Optimist pram," a popular tiny trainer for youngsters. The lateen is also rare in these waters except for a variation that is often used on *board boats** like the "Sunfish" or "Sailfish."

Gaff and Marconi sails are by far the most often seen sails today. Of these two, the Marconi, sometimes called *jib-headed*, is the more modern type and is gradually replacing the gaff. The Marconi sail has many advantages over the gaff: the rigging is simpler and easier to handle; there is less weight and windage

---

*Board boats—Flat board-like boats having little depth and having a very shallow cockpit, if any.

FIGURE 10: COMMON FORE & AFT RIGS

A. MAINSAIL B. JIB C. FORESAIL
D. FORE STAYSAIL E. MIZZEN

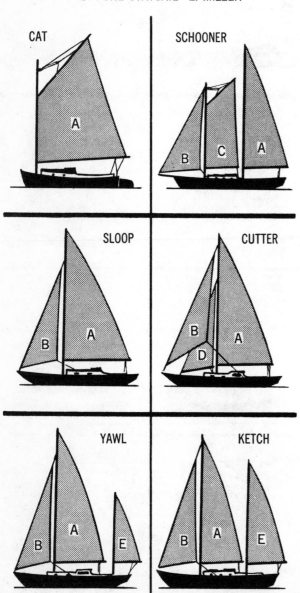

aloft*; the sail is higher to catch high breezes in calm weather; and there is little sagging off of the upper sail area, enabling the boat to sail closer to the wind.

The most common fore and aft rigs made up of Marconi or gaff sails are illustrated in Figure 10. They are the cat, sloop, cutter, yawl, ketch, and schooner.

The cat, the simplest of all rigs, has but one sail, often a gaff, and one mast which is located in the extreme bow of the boat. This sail is called the *mainsail* (pronounced mains'l), which is the name given to the largest sail on a fore and aft vessel having less than three masts. Though the cat is a simple rig and is used successfully on small dinghies (undecked rowing types), it has some disadvantages on larger boats in that the mast is difficult to stay and cat boats often have a fierce weather helm. Also, with this rig, sail cannot be reduced in a blow except by *reefing**.

Other fore and aft rigs with one mast are the sloop and cutter. On these the sail area is divided between the mainsail and one or two sails forward of the mast. Attached to a stay at the bow, the sail farthest forward is called the *jib* (see Figure 10). Sloops and cutters differ partly in the position of the mast, with a cutter's being located farther aft, usually at least two-fifths of the waterline length aft. Cutters generally have smaller mainsails than sloops. The other feature that distinguishes a cutter from a sloop is that the former has at least two *headsails* (sails forward of the mast). The one farthest aft is called the *fore staysail*.

Yawls and ketches are quite similar. Each has two masts, the larger, called the mainmast, being forward and a smaller mast, called the mizzenmast, aft. The difference in these two rigs lies chiefly in the size and location of the *mizzen*, the sail hoisted on the mizzenmast. A ketch's mizzen is much larger and usually farther forward than a yawl's. Technically speaking, a ketch's mizzen must be forward of the *rudder head* or top of the rudder; however, this is not a very satisfactory distinction since some yawl-rigged boats might have *outboard rudders** which, by this definition, would make them ketches. For all practical purposes, it is the relative size and position of the mizzen which distinguishes these two rigs. The mizzen on a yawl is approximately one-quarter the area of her main, while on a ketch, it is approximately two-thirds of her mainsail area.

The schooner was, until modern times, the most

---

*Aloft—High off the deck on the mast or in the rigging.

*Reefing—A method of reducing sail by either tying the shortened sail to its boom or by rolling the sail around its boom, foot, or luff (see details in Section XI).

*Outboard rudders—Rudders which are abaft the hull being attached to transom or stern post of a double-ended or sharp-sterned boat (see Fig. 7, A and C).

popular fore and aft rig in America. On work boats the schooner rig has had as many as seven masts; but on yachts there are almost always two masts, with the smaller—called the *foremast*—forward and the larger mainmast aft. Most contemporary schooner yachts have a gaff foresail and Marconi main, but some have their foresail set on a stay running from high on the mainmast to the base of the foremast, and they are called *staysail schooners.*

Any divided rig such as the sloop, cutter, yawl, ketch, or schooner has an advantage in that its sail area may be reduced by the removal of one or a combination of sails without reefing. These rigs are most suitable for large boats because no one sail need be too large to handle easily.

Cutters, sloops, and yawls seem to be the most popular rigs today, primarily, I think, because of the great current interest in yacht racing. These rigs enable a boat to sail closer to the wind than the ketch and schooner rigs, and since almost every race has a *windward leg**, close-windedness is desirable. Schooners excel when the wind is on their beam, but their short foremast prevents them from carrying very large *spinnakers*, balloon-like racing sails used when running before the wind. The ketch rig seems to lend itself more to cruising and offshore sailing than to racing, although there are a few racing ketches having large mizzenmasts stepped far aft. The ketch is one of the most versatile rigs, having a great number of sail combinations. The vessel with this rig may have her sail area *shortened* or reduced with maximum ease.

BALANCE

Balance is the relationship of a boat's sail plan to her *center of lateral resistance* (C.L.R.) and determines whether a boat has a tendency to head up into the wind when her helm is left alone or whether she will head off, away from the wind. The former tendency is called a *weather helm*, while the latter is called a *lee helm*. A boat's center of lateral resistance is the theoretical central point on the hull's underwater silhouette at which the boat can be pushed sideways without turning. This point may be found simply by cutting out the underwater silhouette from stiff cardboard and balancing it from a pin (Figure 11). The side view of a boat's sail also has a point of balance or geometric center which is called the *center of effort*. A combination of the centers of effort of each sail in the sail plan lies at a point called the *total center of effort* (T.C.E.). This total center of effort is nearly always designed to lead

Windward leg—Course against the wind.

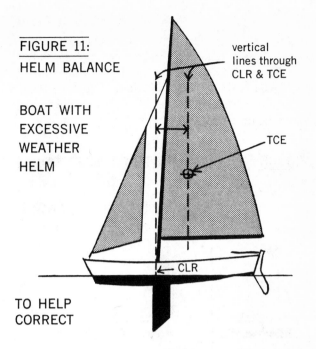

FIGURE 11: HELM BALANCE

BOAT WITH EXCESSIVE WEATHER HELM

vertical lines through CLR & TCE

TCE

CLR

TO HELP CORRECT

1 PREVENT HEELING TO LEEWARD
2 MOVE WEIGHT AFT
3 RAISE CENTERBOARD SLIGHTLY
4 RAKE MAST FORWARD
5 TRIM JIB SHEET (PULL IT IN) OR SET LARGER JIB
6 REDUCE AREA OF MAINSAIL OR HAVE IT RECUT TO REDUCE DRAFT (SEE FIG. 16) NEAR AFTER EDGE

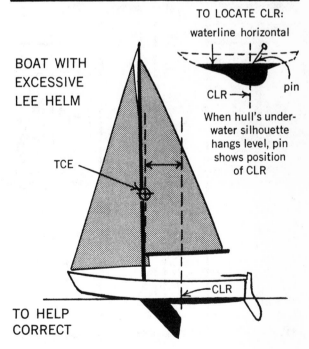

BOAT WITH EXCESSIVE LEE HELM

TCE

CLR

TO LOCATE CLR:
waterline horizontal

CLR

pin

When hull's underwater silhouette hangs level, pin shows position of CLR

TO HELP CORRECT

1 HEEL TO LEEWARD
2 MOVE WEIGHT FORWARD
3 LOWER CENTERBOARD
4 RAKE MAST AFT
5 EASE (SLACK) JIB SHEET OR SET SMALLER JIB
6 ENLARGE MAIN AND/OR TIGHTEN ITS LEECH (AFTER EDGE)

slightly the center of lateral resistance. On most normal boats this lead is about 10 to 20 percent of the waterline length. If the total center of effort were much farther forward, the boat would have a lee helm, while if the T.C.E. were abaft the C.L.R., her weather helm would be excessive.

FIGURE 12: BALANCE WITH REDUCED SAIL

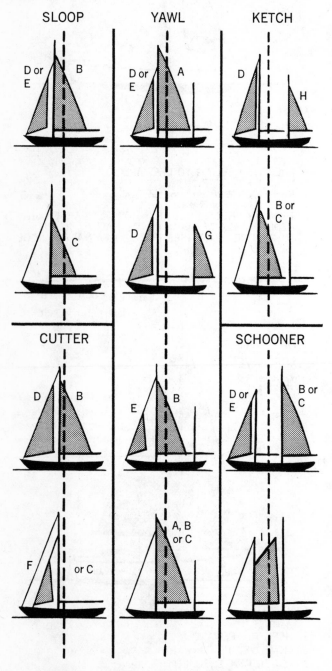

BROKEN LINES ARE TCE UNDER FULL SAIL

A. full mainsail B. reefed main C. deeply reefed main D. jib
E. storm jib F. staysail G. mizzen H. reefed mizzen I. foresail

Every properly designed sailboat should, in a light breeze, have a very slight weather helm. This makes sailing easier because it gives the helmsman a *feel** through the light, consistent pull of the tiller. Also, a slight weather helm is a built-in safety device, for it causes a boat to *luff up* or head into the wind, losing headway and gaining stability in the event that the helmsman should let go of the tiller. As mentioned, however, this weather helm should only be slight in a light breeze because as the wind freshens and as the average boat increases her angle of heel, so will her weather helm increase. Thus if a boat has a strong tendency to head up in light airs, her weather helm will be excessive in heavy breezes.

Some boats have either too much or too little weather helm. Figure 11 attempts to show the causes of these faults and how to correct them. Of course, if these helm faults are extreme, the entire sail plan should be redesigned with the mast moved forward to correct the weather helm or moved aft to correct the lee helm. However, unless the boat is very poorly designed, less drastic measures such as *raking** the mast, setting smaller or larger sails, shifting ballast, and raising or lowering the centerboard will nearly always be sufficient to make helm corrections. To maintain proper sail balance when reefing or shortening down, sail areas on either side of the total center of effort should be reduced almost equally so that the area on one side will balance the area on the other side, as shown in Figure 12. Actually, somewhat more sail should be carried forward as the wind increases to help correct for the weather helm caused by excessive heeling.

RIGGING

A boat's *rigging* consists of the stays and lines used for the support and control of her rig. The rigging used for support is called *standing rigging* and is composed of the permanent stays used to hold up or keep straight a mast or spar; the rigging used for sail control is *running rigging* and is used to pull in, pull up, or adjust the sails. Nowadays, standing rigging is almost always made entirely of metal wire, usually stainless steel, but running rigging is at least partly rope and sometimes entirely rope.

Figure 13 shows two different standing rigging plans for a sloop. A is a masthead plan with the forward stay, called the *head stay*, going to the top of the mast. This is a simple, logical arrangement for a boat which is not

Feel—A communication through the sense of touch on the helm which tells the helmsman how his boat is responding to wind and water.

Rake—Inclination from the perpendicular of a mast (see Fig. 11).

FIGURE 13: STANDING RIGGING & SUGGESTIONS FOR TUNING

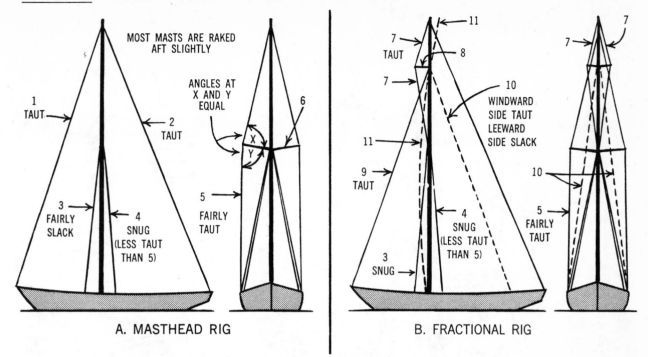

A. MASTHEAD RIG

B. FRACTIONAL RIG

1 HEAD STAY 2 PERMANENT BACKSTAY 3 FORWARD LOWER SHROUD 4 AFTER LOWER
SHROUD 5 UPPER SHROUD 6 SPREADER 7 JUMPER STAY 8 JUMPER STRUT
9 JIB STAY 10 RUNNING BACKSTAYS 11 MAST BOWED TO FLATTEN SAIL FOR HEAVY WINDS

NOTE: It is recommended that the beginning sailor keep his mast straight. However, if the mast is bowed, it should be bowed as shown by dotted line II with the mast's top (above jib stay) bending aft and the mast's middle (below jib stay's intersection with the mast) bending forward. This will remove draft or flatten mainsail, which is desirable in heavy winds. When the mast has a head stay, or when sails are cut for straight mast, or in light airs, the mast should be bent relatively little if at all. Bend is controlled mainly by adjusting jumpers and permanent backstay.

too large, for it allows the use of a large jib and enables the after stay, called the *permanent backstay*, to pull back at a point on the mast directly behind the head stay, thus preventing the mast from being unintentionally bent. Sloop B has a *fractional rig* with a slightly shorter forward stay, called the *jib stay*, fastened to the mast below the backward pull of her permanent backstay; *jumper stays* and *jumper struts* have been added to the forward side of the mast to prevent it from being bent back excessively. Large boats with this arrangement might also need *running backstays* (shown by dotted lines), which attach to the mast behind the jib stay and require *setting up* (tightening) or *slacking off* (loosening) on certain points of sailing. Side stays running from the mast down to the sides are called *shrouds*, and the side arms that hold them out from the mast are called *spreaders*.

Tuning or properly adjusting the standing rigging is a complicated and often controversial procedure for the sophisticated racing man, but since this book is primar-

ily for the beginning sailor, I shall only touch upon this lightly. Standing rigging may be adjusted by means of the *turnbuckle* (shown in Figure 14, M), which is attached to the bottom of a stay. The shroud turnbuckles are secured to *chain-plates*, metal straps which run down the side of a boat, occasionally on the hull's exterior but usually on the inside of the planking. Racing sailors often like their rigging set up tight, but the casual sailor, particularly the beginner, should carry his stays only moderately taut, because tight rigging exerts a tremendous strain on a boat. The mast's downward thrust is considerable, and the upward pull by the shrouds can open a boat's seams and after a number of years cause the boat to become *hogged*, or look humpbacked. Upper shrouds should be carried a little more taut than the lowers to keep the mast's top from bending to leeward. It is perfectly natural to have the *lee* shrouds, those away from the wind, quite slack when the boat's angle of heel is pronounced. In this situation, the windward shrouds, up-

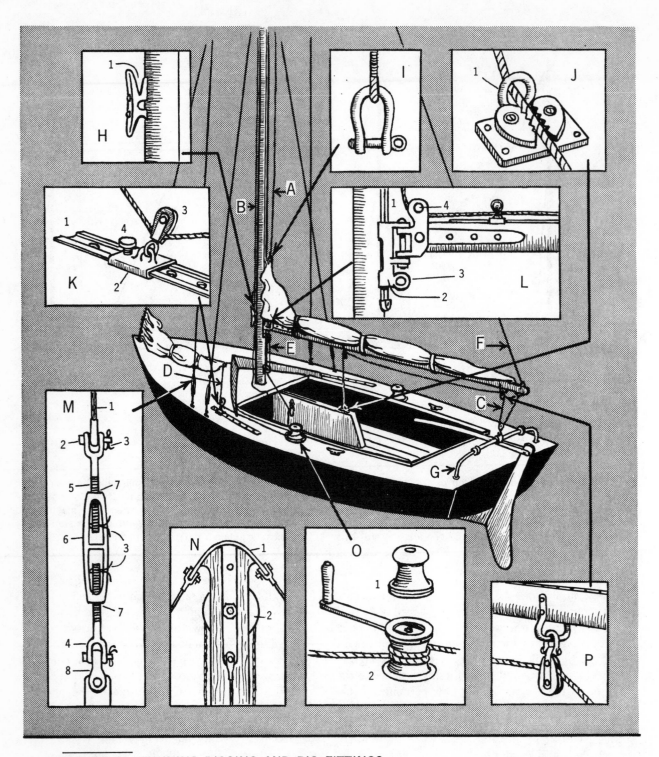

FIGURE 14: RUNNING RIGGING AND RIG FITTINGS

A MAIN HALYARD (cleats on mast's starboard side)

B JIB HALYARD (cleats on mast's port side)

C MAIN SHEET

D JIB SHEET

E DOWNHAUL

F TOPPING LIFT

G TRAVELER

H JAM CLEAT
(1) narrow space in which line is jammed (see fig. 29)

I SCREW SHACKLE (a reliable type)

J CAM-ACTION CLEAT
(1) fair lead (often has block, as in K, instead of ring fair lead)

K ADJUSTABLE LEAD FOR JIB SHEET
(1) track (2) slide
(3) swivel block (pulley)
(4) adjustable thumb screw

L SLIDING GOOSENECK
(1) track (2) slide
(3) attachment for downhaul
(4) tack pin

wind, on the high side, will be taut, taking all the lateral strain.

Head stays and jib stays should be kept reasonably taut because a sagging stay to which a jib is attached will hurt a boat's ability to *point* or sail close to the wind. Although some boats, particularly those with a lot of *draft* or fullness in their mainsail, carry a bend aft in their mast at times, the average boat with a normally cut mainsail, cut for a straight mast, should have her mast straight, as a bend or twist might destroy the sail's proper shape causing wrinkles or *hard spots**. Jumper stays should lead far enough down the mast so the turnbuckles are accessible from the deck. The amount of bow (bending) aft is controlled mainly by the adjustment of these stays and/or backstays.

Principal lines in the running rigging are *halyards*, which pull sails up; sheets, which pull sails in; *outhauls*, which pull sails out on their boom; *downhauls*, which pull sails down; and *topping lifts*, which hold booms up when the sails are down. These lines are shown on the small sloop in Figure 14, together with their related fittings. Cleats are used to make fast the lines or secure them. *Jam cleats* require only one complete wrap around with the line jamming under the narrowly spaced end. A *winch* is used to pull in on a line when it is under strain. The line is wrapped several times around the winch drum clockwise and the handle is wound around to pull in a sheet or halyard. The rest of these details are self-explanatory in the diagram.

---

*Hard spots—Areas of a sail that are stretched flat, not properly curved.

M TURNBUCKLE
   (1) shroud (2) clevis pin
   (3) cotter pin (should be wrapped in tape)
   (4) clevis (5) threads
   (6) barrel (turn to tighten stay)
   (7) some turnbuckles have locknuts here instead of cotter pins
   (8) toggle (should be on large boats at head stay to prevent metal fatigue at clevis)

N MASTHEAD FITTINGS
   (1) tang (for shroud or stay attachment)
   (2) halyard sheave (after end should project to hold top of sail slightly away from mast)

O WINCHES
   (1) snubbing winch (without handle) for small boats
   (2) ratchet winch (removeable handle) for large boats

P BOOM BAIL WITH BLOCK

NOTE: All fittings should be through-bolted wherever possible.

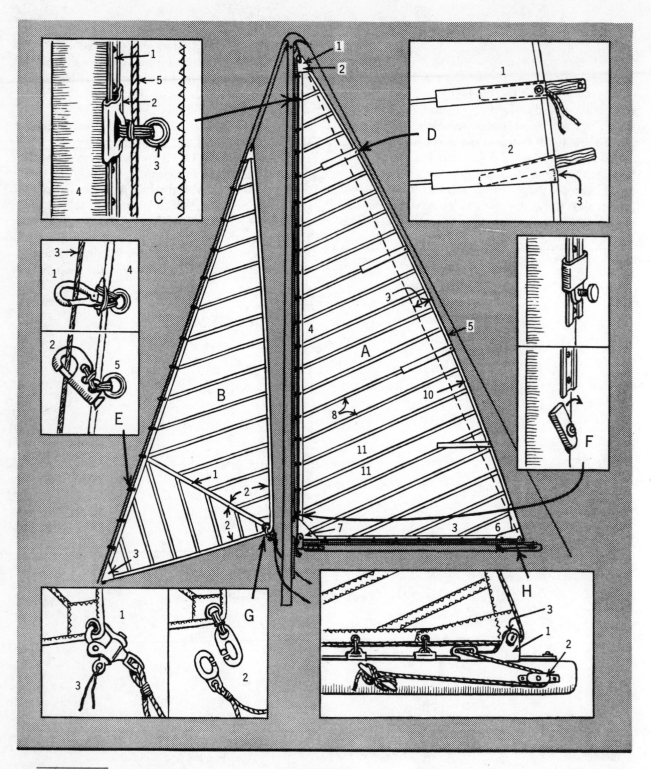

FIGURE 15: WORKING SAILS & RELATED FITTINGS

A MARCONI CROSS-CUT
   MAINSAIL
   (1) head (2) headboard
   (3) foot (4) luff (5) leech
   (6) clew (7) tack (8) seams
   (9) roach (10) tabling
   (11) cloths

B MITER-CUT JIB
   (1) miter seam
   (2) angle between foot
       and miter seam is equal
       to angle between leech
       and miter seam
   (3) corner patch

C SAIL SLIDE OR CAR
   (1) track (2) slide (3) grommet
       small shackle may be used to
       secure slide to grommet.
   (4) mast (5) bolt rope

D BATTENS & BATTEN POCKETS
   (1) conventional type with lanyards
   (2) offset pocket sewn closed at (3)

SAILS

MATERIALS

Just prior to World War II, the commonly used material for sails was cotton, with Egyptian cotton considered the best. At present, however, virtually all yacht sails are made from synthetic cloths such as nylon, Mylar, Kevlar, and especially polyester, called Dacron in the United States. For most sails Dacron is hard to beat. Compared with cotton it is highly resistant to stretch, shrinkage, mildew, and sun rot. As compared with Mylar and Kevlar, Dacron is quite stable, but it is less expensive, easier to handle, and generally more durable. An early, relatively elastic synthetic cloth is nylon, which is ideal for the *parachute spinnaker*, a very full sail shaped like an isosceles triangle, suspended by three corners only, and intended for reaching or running (see Section VIII). Nylon can be obtained in very light weights to prevent the spinnaker from collapsing in light airs, and its moderate elasticity alleviates shock loading and excessive rigidity which may cause the sail to bounce too much in choppy seas. On the other hand, elasticity and stretch are highly undesirable characteristics for any sail that is carried upwind. It must be sufficiently heavy, rigid, and stable to resist stretching that results from extreme loading due to flat sheeting (maximum trimming) in fresh winds. With sufficient weight of cloth, Dacron is reasonably stable. In light weights its resistance to stretch can be optimized on expensive racing sails by combining or reinforcing it with Kevlar or Mylar.

Stretch can be minimized not only by using stable materials but also with cloth finishing processes and the sail's cut or manner of orienting the cloth panels during construction. The finishing processes include various methods of treating the cloth with heat, pressure (under rollers), and resin filler or coatings. Unless subjected to extreme wear and stress, resinated sails are very stable, but they are also stiff, slippery, and generally difficult to handle. For the nonracing sailor I would advise choosing a moderately heavy, soft cloth with minimum resin not only for easier handling but also because of its better ability to recover if it should happen to be overloaded and stretched out of shape.

BENDING ON SAILS

Figure 15 shows the sails on a sloop with their proper nomenclature and important details. The diagram shows how a sail is secured to the mast, boom, and jib stay. The jib is fastened to the stay by snap hooks or *hanks*. In bending on this sail, we begin by shackling down its *tack* or bottom forward corner. Then we snap on the hanks (two different kinds are shown in the diagram), working our way up from the tack to the *head* or top of the sail. Next we shackle the jib halyard to the jib's head and shackle the jib sheets on to the jib's *clew* or after, bottom corner. (The usual type of snap shackle for jib halyards and sheets is shown in Figure 15.) Some sailors prefer to tie on their jib sheets with *bowlines* (knots illustrated in Figure 69).

On most Marconi-rigged boats, all working sails except jibs and staysails are held to the boom and mast by *sail slides* or cars, as shown in the diagram. These cars are slid onto a track which is secured to the after side of the mast and top of the boom. In bending on a mainsail or mizzen, it is necessary to start with the head. First the halyard is fastened to the *headboard**,

---

*Headboard—Stiff plate of metal or wood sewn to the head of a Marconi sail.

E **JIB HANKS (two types)**
   (1) snap hook (2) piston hank
   (3) head stay or jib stay
   (4) jib (5) grommet

F **SLIDE STOPS (two types)**
   to keep slides or cars from
   sliding off track when you
   wish to lower mainsail but
   not remove it from mast

G **JIB CLEW SHACKLES**
   (two types)
   (1) snap shackle
   (2) Brummel or Inglefield hooks
      (hooks interlock when
      placed at right angles
      to each other)
   (3) lashing cord (spring-loaded pin
      on snap shackle should be lashed
      in because it can open when
      jib flaps violently)

H **OUTHAUL FITTING**
   (1) outhaul slide
   (2) cheek block (3) clew pin

NOTE: Sails are made to have a curve or belly from luff to leech called camber or draft (see fig. 16). Draft is built into a sail by giving its luff and foot a slight roach - also by slightly tapering the cloths or varying the width of seams.

quite often with a screw shackle (Figure 14). (Be sure the shackle pin is screwed in tight, because if it should come out with the sail hoisted, the sail would come down and make it necessary for someone to go aloft to retrieve the halyard.) Now we slide the top car on the sail's *luff*, or forward edge, onto the mast track and follow this procedure with the next cars until they are all on the track. Then we adjust the *car stop* (two different types are shown in the diagram) to keep the cars from sliding back off the track. Next we secure the tack, which is the sail's lower, forward corner. Now, we are ready to bend the *foot* or the sail's bottom edge onto the boom. We run the foot through our hands from tack to clew until we come to the aftermost foot slide to see that it's not twisted. We feed this onto the boom track and follow with the other slides as with the luff slides on the mast. Next we slide the sail out to the after end of the boom and secure its clew to the outhaul, as shown in the diagram. Some boats have grooved booms with no track, and occasionally some small boats have grooved masts with no track. In this case the sail has no cars, but instead the *bolt ropes* (ropes sewn to a sail around its edges) are fed into the slot or groove.

I shall not go into the details of bending on a gaff sail, which is a much more complicated procedure, because these sails are much less common today, and once bent on, they are usually left on for the whole season. Marconi sails, however, are usually taken off after every day's sail to preserve them, unless the sail is extremely large and difficult to bend or unbend. Gaff sails are usually secured to wooden hoops on the mast and laced with light line to the gaff (the upper spar) and boom. These sails are hoisted by two lines—the *peak halyard*, which hoists the *peak* or top of the gaff, and the *throat halyard*, which hoists the gaff's bottom or *throat*.

CUT AND SHAPE

Although the cuts of modern racing sails look extremely complicated, all cloth panel orientations are variations or combinations of basic arrangements that align the seams approximately parallel or at right angles to the greatest loads. The reason for this is to avoid harmful bias elongation or stretch that results when the load is diagonal to the weave or thread line. Bias elongation is easily demonstrated by pulling on the corners of a square handkerchief. When diagonally opposite corners are pulled apart, there will be noticeable stretch, but when opposite corners on the same edge are pulled apart, there will be relatively little stretch because the force is parallel and at right angles to the weave. The greatest loads on sails usually occur at the clew and along the *leech* or after edge, and these are areas that especially need reinforcement and panel

alignment that minimizes bias elongation. An increasingly used solution to the problem of corner stretch is the use of radial seams, those radiating from the corner inward toward the center of the sail.

Two of the most commonly used cuts for *working sails** are shown in Figure 15. The mainsail illustrated is *cross-cut*, that is to say its cloth panels are aligned so that the seams and thread lines are at right angles to the leech. Although the seams meet the luff and foot at angles that allow some bias stretch, this can be used to advantage in shaping the sail as illustrated in Figure 16. The typical mainsail (or other sail that is bent to a mast) nearly always has a pronounced *roach* or outward curving of the leech which gives the sail more area. To hold out the roach and keep the leech from curling, which would have a harmful aerodynamic effect, it is necessary to use *battens*, thin wooden, plastic, or fiberglass strips at the leech. These strips are inserted into pockets that are sewn to the leech. Battens are secured in their pockets with *lanyards**, or with the offset opening shown in Figure 15, *D*. There should be elastic sewn into the front end of an offset pocket to keep tension on the batten so that it won't work its way out. When fiberglass battens are used, their inner ends should be fitted with soft vinyl end caps to prevent chafe.

Another popular cut for modern sails is the *miter-cut*. This form of sail construction is generally used for most jibs and staysails (see the jib in Figure 15). The miter-cut is sometimes used also on mainsails, more often on small sailing dinghies. With this cut, a pronounced roach may be given to the foot of the sail which will add to its area. One can see by looking at the diagram that on this type of sail a diagonal seam called the *miter seam* runs from the clew up to the luff. Other seams, running at right angles to the leech and foot, intersect the miter seam.

Figure 16 shows the proper curvature or draft that a sail should have. Sails with incorrect draft are also shown for comparison. Notice that on the correct sails, the greatest curvature is forward near the luff, but not to the extreme of the sail in diagram *D*. The leech should be moderate also, not too tight or too loose. In light airs a sail should have more draft, but in heavy winds it should be flatter. Draft may be adjusted to some extent by merely tightening the outhaul (if the sail has a boom) and the downhaul or halyard to flatten the sail and by slacking the outhaul and downhaul or halyard to give more draft. These adjustments should not be so tight or so slack, however, that prom-

---

Working sails—Sails carried all the time, not just for racing. These do not include the spinnaker or other light sails.
Lanyards—Short pieces of light line used for lashing or securing.

FIGURE 16: SAIL DRAFT AND LUFF AND FOOT ADJUSTMENTS

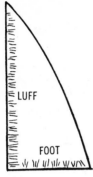

WRINKLES AT RIGHT ANGLES TO LUFF & FOOT

LUFF

FOOT

HALYARD OR DOWNHAUL AND OUTHAUL—TOO SLACK

WRINKLES PARALLEL TO LUFF & FOOT

TOO TIGHT

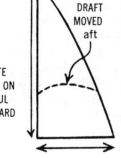

DRAFT MOVED aft

MODERATE TENSION ON DOWNHAUL OR HALYARD

EXTRA TENSION ON OUTHAUL

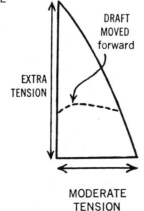

DRAFT MOVED forward

EXTRA TENSION

MODERATE TENSION

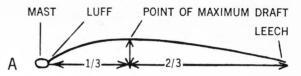

MAST   LUFF   POINT OF MAXIMUM DRAFT   LEECH

A   1/3   2/3

moderate draft with point of maximum draft between 1/3 and 1/2 of distance from luff to leech
GOOD for beating in fresh winds and moderate seas

B

considerable draft with point of maximum draft farther aft
GOOD in light airs and for sailing downwind in all breezes

C

not much draft with point of maximum draft fairly far forward
GOOD in fresh breezes, effective when sailing to windward

D

draft too far forward
BAD for sailing close to the wind, particularly with an overlapping jib. Draft might be moved slightly farther aft by tightening outhaul and slacking downhaul

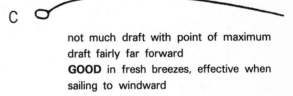

E

draft too far aft and leech is too tight (curves too far inboard)
BAD anytime, especially in fresh wind. Draft might be improved slightly by tightening downhaul and/or halyard

F

leech too slack
BAD at all times, especially in light airs

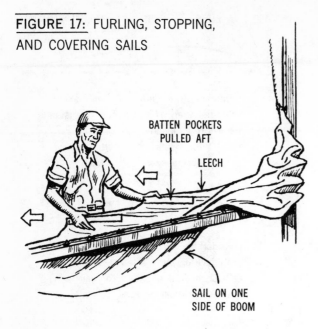

BATTEN POCKETS PULLED AFT

LEECH

SAIL ON ONE SIDE OF BOOM

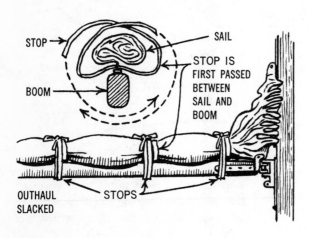

STOP

BOOM

SAIL

STOP IS FIRST PASSED BETWEEN SAIL AND BOOM

OUTHAUL SLACKED

STOPS

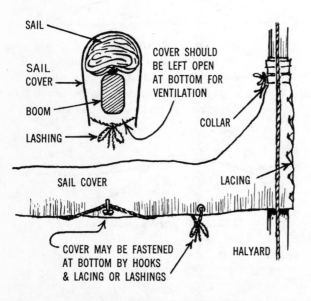

SAIL

SAIL COVER

BOOM

LASHING

COVER SHOULD BE LEFT OPEN AT BOTTOM FOR VENTILATION

COLLAR

SAIL COVER

LACING

COVER MAY BE FASTENED AT BOTTOM BY HOOKS & LACING OR LASHINGS

HALYARD

inent wrinkles occur along the foot and luff. This is explained in Figure 16.

CARE OF SAILS

Modern synthetic sails are tough, but they need proper care for the most effective use over a long period of time. The life of an expensive sail can be shortened by lengthy exposure to the sun, chafe, excessive flapping, and stress from overloading. The latter takes place most often when a lightweight sail is carried in winds much stronger than those for which it is designed, especially when it is sheeted flat and stretched out of shape. Loss of optimal shape can also result when the luff is repeatedly stretched extremely tight with a powerful halyard winch or from repeated failure to slack the outhaul when a sail is left bent on a boom. Never leave an edge of a sail under great tension for long periods of time.

Continuous flapping, in a strong breeze especially, tends to fatigue, wear, or break the threads of any cloth. For this reason avoid prolonged heading into the wind with sails hoisted and don't dry sails by leaving them hoisted in windy weather. Chafe is best avoided with patches or protective cloth strips wherever the sail rubs against the rigging. It is especially important to apply chafing patches to vulnerable seams because wear can rapidly destroy the stitching. Any objects, such as spreader tips, that rub against a sail need padding with soft material or rubber boots.

To avoid excessive exposure to the sun, sails should be unbent and kept in bags whenever possible. If the sail is made of stiff Dacron, it is best that it be folded before being bagged. A jib that is stuffed in a bag should be stowed with its tack on top (near the bag's mouth) so that it can quickly be found when the sail is bent on again. Sails that are left bent on must be properly furled and protected with sail covers from rain, bird droppings, and especially damaging ultraviolet rays. A roller furling jib usually has sail cover or sun-resistant material sewn to its leech and foot so that the sail will automatically be protected when the sail is rolled up.

Figure 17 shows the furling, stopping, and covering of a typical mainsail. After sail is lowered, it should be pulled entirely over on either side of the boom. Then the leech is lifted up and pulled aft so that the battens lie parallel to the boom. Next, the *bunt* or loose bulk in the center of the sail is bundled into the hammock-like space between the leech and boom, and the sail is rolled up snugly till it lies in a neat roll on top of the boom. *Stops* or short strips of cloth are used to hold the furled sail on the boom. When the foot is secured to the boom with slides on a track, the stops can most effectively be used if they are inserted between the foot and boom. Sometimes this is even done before the sail is lowered. Then the stop is passed over the furled sail, pulled tight, passed down under the boom, and brought back up to the top of the sail and made fast. Sail covers are then put on. These are specially fitted covers usually made of vinyl or acrylic fabric. The latter is ideal, as it is highly resistant to ultraviolet degradation and is not so waterproof that air will not pass through the material. Sails must be allowed to "breathe" under a cover, otherwise they will become mildewed. For this reason, covers should not be laced too tight under the boom. They are secured by a system of hooks or lashings. It is important that the cover's collar or top part, which goes around the mast, is tied tight and if possible to have the halyards outside the collar, because otherwise rainwater may run down the mast under the collar and soak the sail. Even though synthetic sails are not damaged by mildew they can become unsightly. The most important function of a cover is to protect against bird droppings and especially sun rot.

Try to avoid bagging or covering a sail when it is wet. If this must be done, dry the sails by spreading them on deck or hoisting them in light airs. Remember not to let them flap excessively for long periods of time. Sails can be washed, but never put them in a home washing machine because of its violent agitation. Use a mild soap and moderately warm water, and never use an abrasive scrubber. If a small tear or rip appears in a sail, it can be temporarily stopped with sticky sail tape or sewing, but see your sailmaker as soon as possible. The most common cause of snagged sails is *cotter pins* (see Figure 14, *M*). Be sure that every cotter pin is thoroughly wrapped in waterproof tape. In some cases it might be covered with a glob of silicone before being taped.

THE THEORY OF SAILING

The actual sailing of a boat is more an art than a science, and therefore it can really be learned only by practice. However, the beginner will find a simple study of the theory of sailing invaluable. Before getting under way for the first time, he should have a fair understanding of the following: how to determine wind direction, general sail positions, and points of sailing; turning maneuvers; elementary aerodynamics or how the wind moves his boat; and the trim of sails.

WIND DIRECTION

The beginner must accustom himself to knowing, at all times, from which direction the wind is blowing, for this determines how his sails are to be trimmed and in what direction his boat is able to move. There are certain signs of wind direction. Boats *moored** in a harbor without excessive tidal currents will always point into the wind when anchored from the bow. Smoke and flags will be blown away from the wind. Also, small ripples will move across the top of the water with the wind. Many boats are equipped with a *masthead fly* or vane (Figure 18) for the determining of wind direction. A good substitute is a *telltale* or light piece of yarn or

---

*Moored—Secured to a permanent-type anchor; see Section IX.

thread tied to a shroud about six feet or more above the deck. Experienced sailors can tell which way the wind is blowing by the feel of it on face or neck. In very light airs, they sometimes wet a finger and hold it up in the air. Even the slightest zephyr will make the finger cooler on its side facing the breeze.

POINTS OF SAILING

There are three general points of sailing, or directions in which a boat may move with respect to the wind. These are *running, reaching,* and *beating,* and they are explained in Figure 19. Running is that point of sailing when the wind is behind or is blowing from astern. It is also called *sailing free, sailing downwind, off the wind, before the wind,* or *scudding.* Reaching is sailing across the wind or with the wind on the boat's side. Courses on this point of sailing are more specifically identified by the *close reach,* when the wind is coming from forward of the beam; the *beam reach,* when the wind is directly on the beam; and the *broad reach,* when the wind is more on the quarter. Beating is sailing as close to the wind as possible. This is often called *tacking, sailing to windward, close hauled,* or simply *on the wind.* A boat obviously cannot sail directly into the wind or her sails would merely flap like the family wash and would be totally ineffective; so she has to *bear off*

FIGURE 18: WIND INDICATORS

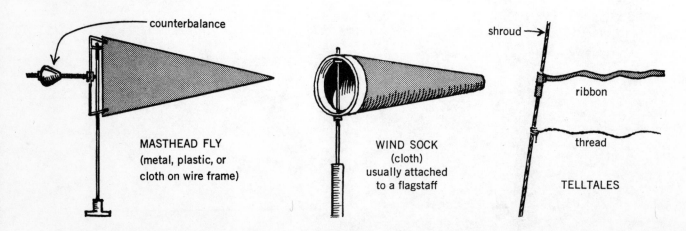

counterbalance

MASTHEAD FLY
(metal, plastic, or
cloth on wire frame)

WIND SOCK
(cloth)
usually attached
to a flagstaff

shroud →

ribbon

thread

TELLTALES

or head away from the wind until her sails, when trimmed in, *fill* or stop flapping. At this point, she is close hauled.

Figure 19 shows drawings of sloops running, reaching, and beating. Opposite each drawing is a diagram which shows the correct boom and sail position for that particular point of sailing. When running, the main sheet is slacked so that the boom is all the way off until it almost touches the after shroud. It should not touch the shroud because the stay would chafe against the boom and scar it. On this point of sailing the driving force is mostly the push of the wind against the sail; thus by *starting* the main sheet or letting it off, as far as possible, the greatest sail area is presented to the wind. Notice the jib on the boat running before the wind in Figure 19. It is hanging limply because on this particular heading with the wind blowing from dead astern, the jib is being blanketed by the mainsail. This simply means that the mainsail is blocking off the wind which would otherwise be blowing on the jib. To put it another way, the jib lies in the mainsail's *wind shadow*.

Reaching is the fastest point of sailing, and there are two kinds of forces working on the sails: the wind's push on the windward side of the sails and its pull by the creation of a suction on the lee side of the sails. On the beam reach, sheets are trimmed so that the sails are about halfway out. On a close reach, sails are trimmed closer, but on a broad reach, they are let off farther than when the boat is beam reaching. If she is moving particularly fast, sheets are trimmed in a little more than usual. This is because of what we call the *apparent wind*, and it is explained in Figure 20. If you are driving along in a car and thrust your hand out the window, you will notice a strong wind coming from ahead. This wind is caused by the car's speed. The same thing is true to a lesser degree with a boat. The boat's forward speed causes the real wind to appear to be blowing from farther ahead. This new wind from a more forward direction is the apparent breeze, and sails must be trimmed in slightly to meet it.

The average boat of modern rig can sail to within about 45 degrees of the wind when beating to windward. Of course a few boats can sail a little closer than this, while others are not able to sail quite as close. In order to get to a windward or upwind destination, a sailboat must make a zigzag course toward her destination. Each leg or heading on this course is called a tack (see Figure 19). When the boat is headed so that the wind blows across her starboard side and her sails are trimmed in over the port side, she is said to be on the *starboard tack*; she is on the *port tack* when the wind blows across her port side and her sails lie to leeward, on the starboard side. When beating to windward, a boat's heading on the starboard tack should be approximately at right angles or 90 degrees to her heading on

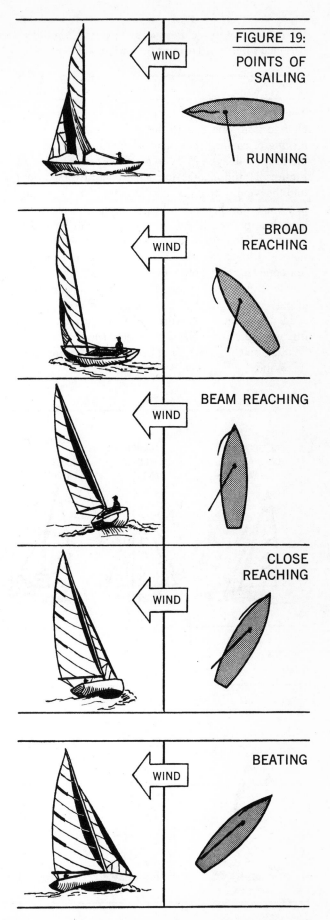

FIGURE 19: POINTS OF SAILING

RUNNING

BROAD REACHING

BEAM REACHING

CLOSE REACHING

BEATING

the port tack. On a close-hauled boat, sails should be trimmed almost as far in as they will come.

TURNS

There are two kinds of turns a sailboat may make to change from one tack to the other. These are called *tacking* or *coming about* and *jibing* (pronounced and often spelled gybing) or *wearing ship,* explained in Figures 21 and 22. Tacking consists of turning a boat into the wind so that her sails flap and then continuing to turn so that her sails fill on the opposite side of the boat. In other words, you are changing your boat from a port tack to starboard tack or vice versa by turning upwind. Jibing, on the other hand, consists of changing from one tack to the other by turning downwind so that in the middle of the turn the wind is blowing from directly astern. In this turn the sails do not flap but suddenly swing across. Turns, as well as points of sailing, will be dealt with in more detail in Section VII, "Sailing on the Wind," and Section VIII, "Sailing Off the Wind."

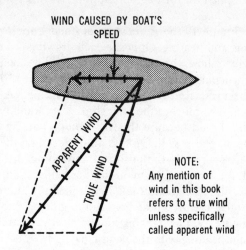

FIGURE 20: APPARENT WIND

WIND CAUSED BY BOAT'S SPEED

APPARENT WIND

TRUE WIND

NOTE:
Any mention of wind in this book refers to true wind unless specifically called apparent wind

If true wind is 9 MPH and boat speed is 4 MPH, then apparent wind is 11 MPH.

FIGURE 21: TACKING

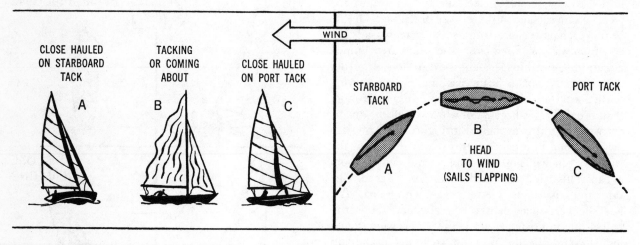

WIND

CLOSE HAULED ON STARBOARD TACK
A

TACKING OR COMING ABOUT
B

CLOSE HAULED ON PORT TACK
C

STARBOARD TACK
A

B
HEAD TO WIND (SAILS FLAPPING)

PORT TACK
C

FIGURE 22: JIBING

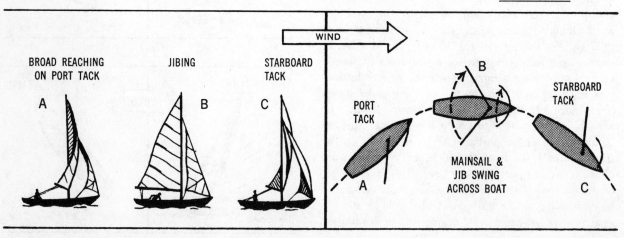

WIND

BROAD REACHING ON PORT TACK
A

JIBING
B

STARBOARD TACK
C

PORT TACK
A

B

MAINSAIL & JIB SWING ACROSS BOAT

STARBOARD TACK
C

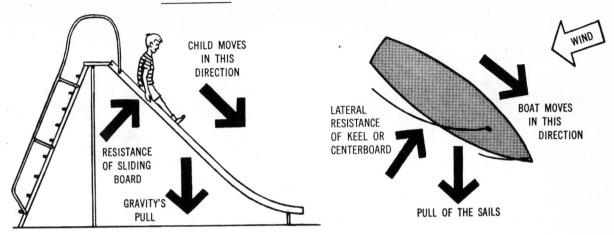

CHILD MOVES IN THIS DIRECTION

RESISTANCE OF SLIDING BOARD

GRAVITY'S PULL

WIND

LATERAL RESISTANCE OF KEEL OR CENTERBOARD

BOAT MOVES IN THIS DIRECTION

PULL OF THE SAILS

BASIC AERODYNAMICS OF SAIL

It is relatively easy to understand how the wind drives a boat when she is running or even broad reaching. This driving force is mostly the wind's push on the windward side of the sails. However, even though man has been sailing for centuries, he has only in modern times been able to comprehend the force that drives a boat to windward. This recent understanding is largely due to the research in aerodynamics which accompanied and followed the invention of the airplane. The forces which lift the wing of a plane, like those which lift the wing of a bird, are similar to those which act on a sail when a boat moves to windward, or against the wind. The chief difference between flying and sailing to windward is that the force which gives a bird or plane its lift is the force which gives a sailboat its forward drive, because the air foil in flight is horizontal, while the sail is vertical. The lift on the top of a wing and the driving force on the lee side of a sail is actually a low pressure pull or suction. On the sailboat this force also tends to pull the boat to leeward, but because of the boat's lateral resistance, supplied, as previously explained, by a keel or centerboard, the suction force will pull the boat ahead. This is explained in Figure 23, which shows the similarity of forces acting on a sailboat to the forces that act against a child on a sliding board.

The suction force or low pressure area on the lee side of a sail is explained by Bernoulli's principle, a law of physics stating that in fluid motion where the velocity of flow is high, the pressure is low. Figure 24 shows a simple physics experiment which demonstrates this principle. Water is forced through a constricted pipe with pressure-indicating tubes in three locations as illustrated. The constricted area in the middle of the

pipe forms a venturi, which speeds up the flow in that region and thus lowers the pressure, causing the water level to be lower in the middle tube. A sail is shaped much like a wing to have camber or curvature (draft). When wind blows against the luff, it will divide into two flows, one traveling toward the leech on the leeward side of the sail and the other flow moving in the same direction but at a slower speed on the windward side. In accordance with Bernoulli's principle, the faster-moving flow will lower the pressure to leeward and cause a suction pull that acts in a somewhat forward direction as shown in Figure 25. Current theory holds that the windward flow is slowed as a result of being partially blocked by circulation currents moving

FIGURE 24: BERNOULLI'S PRINCIPLE

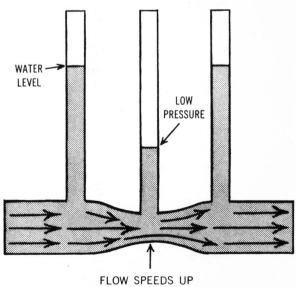

WATER LEVEL

LOW PRESSURE

FLOW SPEEDS UP

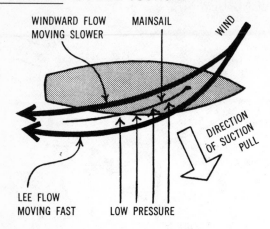

FIGURE 25: LEE-SIDE SUCTION

WINDWARD FLOW MOVING SLOWER

MAINSAIL

WIND

DIRECTION OF SUCTION PULL

LEE FLOW MOVING FAST

LOW PRESSURE

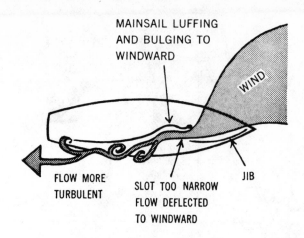

FIGURE 26: JIB BACKWIND

MAINSAIL LUFFING AND BULGING TO WINDWARD

WIND

FLOW MORE TURBULENT

SLOT TOO NARROW FLOW DEFLECTED TO WINDWARD

JIB

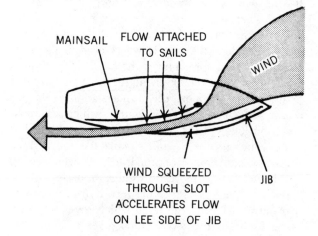

FIGURE 27: A PROPER JIB SLOT

MAINSAIL

FLOW ATTACHED TO SAILS

WIND

WIND SQUEEZED THROUGH SLOT ACCELERATES FLOW ON LEE SIDE OF JIB

JIB

around the sail from leech to luff on the windward side, while the leeward flow is reinforced by the circulation and is therefore accelerated.

Among the functions of a headsail, in addition to adding area and affecting balance, is its ability to interact with the mainsail. Formerly, it was thought that the slot between the mainsail's luff and the jib's leech formed a venturi which forced the wind between the two sails, accelerating the flow over the mainsail. Proponents of the circulation theory, however, feel that most of the benefits from the interaction of the two sails comes from the headsail being helped as a result of the slot speeding up the flow to leeward of the jib while favorably deflecting the wind and diverting more of it to the leeward side.

At any rate, the width of the slot is of great importance. If it is too wide it will lose effectiveness and the flow to leeward of the sails may become detached; but if it is too narrow, the air stream will be directed against the mainsail's lee side, causing it to luff. In this latter case, sailors say that the jib is *backwinding* the main. Backwind is the air that flows off a sail's after edge. This air is very turbulent and disturbing to any sail it blows directly against. Racing skippers use backwind tactically to douse their competitors with turbulent wind. Figure 26 shows a jib which is backwinding the main and causing it to bulge to windward. The exact width of the slot will vary with individual boats and sails. A proper slot would be similar in appearance to that shown in Figure 27. More will be said on this subject in the next section, "Sailing on the Wind."

SAILING ON THE WIND

The beginner should now be ready to see how the actual sailing of a boat is done. We shall move from the general to the particular and look at some of the details and specific procedures involved in beating, reaching, running, tacking, and jibing. This section will deal with all aspects of sailing a boat to windward.

THE HELM

Small sailboats nearly always have a tiller for steering, but boats over 35 or 40 feet in length overall are usually equipped with steering wheels. This is because wheels are designed to give the helmsman a mechanical advantage whereas a tiller exerts a direct pull and it often requires considerable strength to hold it in a hard breeze when a boat develops a weather helm. On a small boat, however, the tiller is generally considered more sensitive; that is, it gives a truer feel to the boat and lets her respond more quickly. In my opinion, most boats over 35 feet L.O.A. (length overall), should have wheels unless they are very finely balanced racing boats, and most well-balanced boats under 35 feet L.O.A. should have tillers.

To turn a boat equipped with a tiller, the helmsman should push the tiller in the opposite direction from the one he wishes his boat to turn. Thus if a boat is moving ahead and the helmsman wants to turn to port, he should push the tiller to starboard, or vice versa. With a wheel, the reverse is true. The helmsman turns the wheel the same way he wishes his boat to turn (like steering an automobile). The beginner should always bear in mind, however, that a boat's turning is caused by the drag of water on one side of the rudder and that to obtain this drag, the boat must be moving through the water. The more slowly a boat is moving, the less efficient is her rudder. When she is standing still, of course, the rudder will not work at all; or, as sailors say, the boat will not answer to her helm. It is therefore very important for the most maneuverability to keep the boat moving at all times.

There are a few instances, as, for example, in leaving a dock or mooring, when a sailor might want his boat to drift backwards. In this case the skipper reverses his helm or, with a tiller, pushes it the same way he wishes his bow to turn—and vice versa with a wheel (see Figure 28). Section IX deals with details of leaving and arriving at docks or moorings.

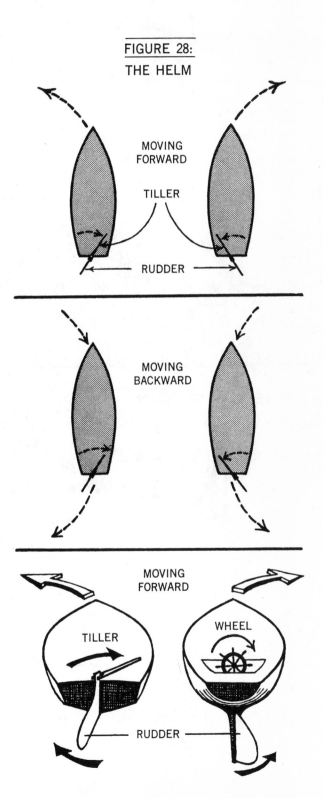

**FIGURE 28:
THE HELM**

MOVING FORWARD

TILLER

RUDDER

MOVING BACKWARD

MOVING FORWARD

TILLER

WHEEL

RUDDER

FIGURE 29: CLEATING THE MAIN SHEET

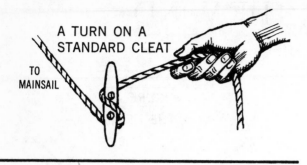

A TURN ON A STANDARD CLEAT

TO MAINSAIL

JAM CLEATS

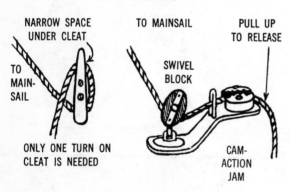

NARROW SPACE UNDER CLEAT

TO MAINSAIL

TO MAINSAIL

PULL UP TO RELEASE

SWIVEL BLOCK

ONLY ONE TURN ON CLEAT IS NEEDED

CAM-ACTION JAM

Also see figure 14

BELAYING ON A STANDARD CLEAT

CRISS-CROSS WRAPS

BEGIN WITH & END WITH A ROUND WRAP

FINISHED WITH A HITCH

A

B

Method B may be used on a halyard but a sheet should never be hitched unless a slippery hitch is used.

SLIPPERY HITCH

TO MAINSAIL

PULL TO UNTIE

BEATING TO WINDWARD

Let us now imagine that we are under way, sailing a small sloop to windward in a light to moderate breeze. You are at the helm with one hand on the tiller and the other on the main sheet while your crew is tending the jib sheets. It is always a good practice to hold in hand the main sheet on a small boat. This is particularly important for a beginner, especially in a centerboard boat that can capsize. With the main sheet in hand, if the boat heels over too far from a strong puff of wind, the mainsail can instantly be slacked so that it will flap, and the boat will gain stability. If you find that holding the main sheet becomes tiresome, you may take a *turn* around the main sheet cleat as shown in Figure 29. On large vessels, sheets may be cleated, but sheets should never be *hitched* on a cleat unless a slippery hitch is used. A hitch and slippery hitch on a cleat are shown in Figure 29. Hitches are sometimes permissible on halyard cleats, but they are apt to jam so they should never be used on a line which might have to be *cast off** in a hurry. Another way to prevent your boat from heeling too far, besides slacking the sheets, is to head her up into the wind. In fact, this should be tried before the sheets are slacked so that the boat may be worked up to windward. Heading up will also cause the sails to luff and the boat to gain stability.

With your hand on the end of the tiller for maximum leverage, you are steering with only two fingers because this boat which you have bought with such care is finely balanced and has only a slight weather helm. Your sheets are pulled in almost as far as they will come. As the breeze lightens, you ease the main off slightly to give your boat a little more drive, but as the wind freshens, you pull in the main slightly, provided the boat doesn't heel too far. You are, of course, sailing to windward, so you are sailing as close to the wind as possible without having the sails luff (ripple at the luff) and thus cause the boat to lose way. The reason for having your sails *flat* or pulled in close on this point of sailing is that the flatter they are, the higher you may point or the closer to the wind you may sail without the sails luffing. In a strong breeze you may carry a slight luff in your main to keep the boat from heeling excessively, but remember that in light and moderate breezes, luffing sails slow down a boat. If your sails are luffing in anything but strong winds, you are either pointing too high or your sails are not trimmed in close enough.

Sailing to windward well requires much practice and great skill, but there is nothing so satisfying. The object is to sail the boat so that she makes the most distance

*Cast off—Let go, untie.

to windward at her best possible speed for this point of sailing. If you bear off or sail away from the wind too far, the boat picks up speed but you lose distance to windward. On the other hand, if you point too high or do what sailors call *pinch* the boat, you gain distance to windward but lose in speed. Even among skilled racing men there are arguments as to whether it pays to pinch a boat slightly or sail her *full and by*, just far enough off the wind to keep her sails completely full. Experienced racing skippers, however, will neither bear off nor pinch excessively. They will always keep their boat moving and pointing reasonably well. Even as a beginner, you are probably already developing a "feel" for your boat so that you sense when she is traveling at her best speed. When she is at her best, she might be sailed still closer to the wind without slowing down, but if she does slow down and begins to feel sluggish, she must be turned slightly away from the wind until she picks up speed again. You should constantly experiment to see if your boat won't point just a little higher yet still keep moving.

Breezes are hardly ever absolutely steady or unvariable. They not only slightly increase and decrease periodically, but frequently shift directions. One moment the breeze might be blowing from more ahead and the next moment from more abeam. If your masthead fly or telltale shows the breeze coming from more abeam, point higher; but if it indicates the breeze is from more ahead, bear off. When a shift of wind permits you to sail higher, it is called a *lift*, but when you must bear off, the shift is called a *header*.

Wind puffs may be seen as dark patches of ripples darting across the water. Even if they do not shift, their velocity increase allows a boat to point higher because the apparent wind draws further aft (see Figure 30). They often radiate somewhat after striking the water, so that as you enter the puff you may be slightly headed at first, but as you pass through the puff you are *let up*, or permitted to sail higher (see Figure 30). When in a good breeze, if the water darkens considerably from a puff, be prepared for a knock down and be ready to *feather up* (head up) so that your boat will stay on her feet and you can work her to windward. You might even have to start to slack your main sheet slightly if she heels a great deal. During the lulls, between the puffs, you should bear off a little to keep your boat moving.

Headers and lifts often occur with great rapidity so that it takes a quickness on the helm to respond to them. Small, light boats may be turned quite rapidly in moderate winds, but with large, heavy boats and any boat in light airs, the helmsman should use a smoother, slower motion in turning. This is because a sudden, violent thrust of a large rudder to one side will act as a brake and slow the boat down. Also, large, heavy boats

FIGURE 30: WIND PUFFS

A puff is a sudden increase in the wind's velocity, usually within a small area and of short duration.

EFFECT OF A PUFF ON APPARENT WIND

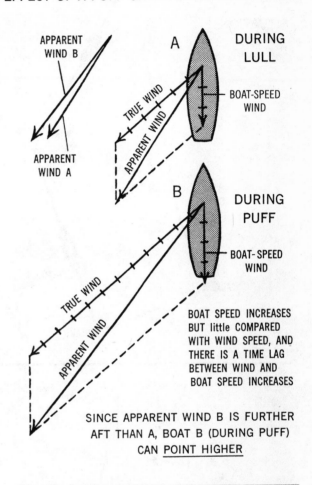

SINCE APPARENT WIND B IS FURTHER AFT THAN A, BOAT B (DURING PUFF) CAN **POINT HIGHER**

THE RADIATING PUFF OR CATSPAW

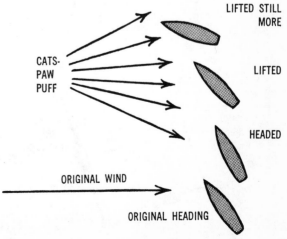

FIGURE 31: WINDWARD STRATEGY

WHENEVER A BOAT IS
SEVERELY HEADED,
SHE SHOULD TACK

SITUATION
A

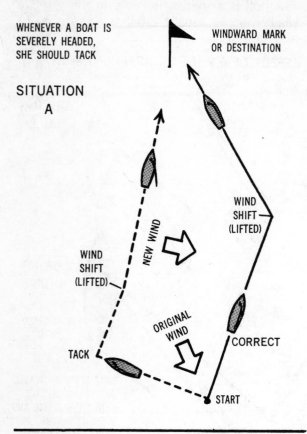

WINDWARD MARK
OR DESTINATION

WIND
SHIFT
(LIFTED)

NEW WIND

WIND
SHIFT
(LIFTED)

ORIGINAL
WIND

CORRECT

TACK

START

SITUATION
B

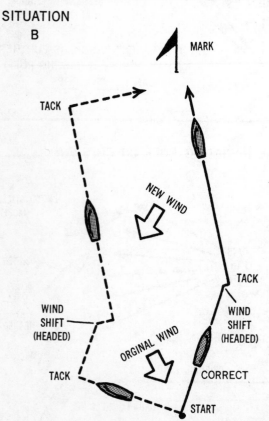

MARK

TACK

NEW WIND

WIND
SHIFT
(HEADED)

TACK

WIND
SHIFT
(HEADED)

ORIGINAL
WIND

CORRECT

TACK

START

are more sluggish and slower to pick up speed once their way has been *killed* or partially stopped.

Whether you are racing or not, there is a proper procedure for getting to your windward destination in the quickest time. Usually your upwind mark or destination will not lie directly to windward but will lie so that you may sail closer to it on one tack than on the other. In this case, you first sail on the tack which permits you to point closest to the windward mark, provided that you are not tacking into more adverse conditions, such as a strong *foul current** or rougher water. The reason for taking the long tack first is that if you get a lift, you might *fetch*, or make your mark without tacking. On the other hand, if you are headed badly, you can come about and come close to fetching on the other tack. This is explained in Figure 31. In this diagram, the solid line courses are the correct ones, while the dotted courses are incorrect. In situation *A*, both boats get a lift which permits them to fetch the mark, but because the boat on the dotted course took the short tack first, her time spent on that tack is almost completely wasted. In situation *B*, both boats get headed. The solid line boat is able to come about and fetch on the next tack, while the dotted line boat is unable to fetch and must tack again. Of course when the wind is absolutely steady, the tack you take first should be determined by the location of a favorable current or other advantageous conditions. But as previously mentioned, most breezes are not absolutely steady but are often quite shifty; so in most instances the long-tack-first rule should be followed.

TACKING

Heretofore you have been sailing along in your sloop on the long tack, but now you see that the windward mark lies off your windward beam so it is time to think about tacking. You should try to pick just the right moment, for if you come about too soon, you may not be able to fetch on the next tack; but if you tack too late, you will *overstand* the mark or travel a superfluous distance on your long tack, thereby wasting time (see Figure 32). Determining the exact moment to tack is often difficult, even for experienced sailors. Most racing skippers will usually favor tacking a bit too soon and gamble that they will get a lift on the next tack, but many cruising skippers would rather overstand slightly than chance having to tack again.

The best way to pick the right moment for tacking is to sight at right angles to the center line of your boat and wait until the mark bears exactly abeam. This is usually the right instant to come about, provided your

---

Foul current—A flow of water against you.

boat will, like most, sail at 45 degrees to the wind when close hauled (discussed in "Points of Sailing," Section VI). Of course, if your boat will point higher you may tack sooner, but if she will not point as high as most boats, you must hold on a bit and tack later.

You now decide that it is time to tack. The correct procedure to follow is to alert your crew by saying. "*Stand by to come about.*" Then he will be ready to cast off the leeward jib sheet and attend to the running backstays if there are any on your boat. The leeward backstay should be slack and the windward one taut. Your next expression will be "*Ready about,*" and this will be followed by "*Hard-a-lee*" or *Helm's-a-lee.*" The latter two expressions mean that the tiller is being pushed to leeward, which would naturally cause the boat to head up into the wind. When your helm is a-lee, it is also said to be *down*; and, of course, the opposite would be true for the helm's being *up*. In this case the boat would be bearing off.

You now shout, "Hard-a-lee," and begin pushing the tiller to leeward. When your sails start to luff, your crew sets up on the leeward backstay that will become the windward backstay. Then when almost head to wind, he slacks the jib sheet and moves over to the other side of the boat where he will slack off the other backstay and take in on the jib's other sheet. As you head into the wind, your sail will be flapping violently; therefore, you and your crew must keep your heads low so as not to be hit by the boom. As your boat begins to fill away on the other tack, the backstay on what is now the leeward side should be slacked and the jib trimmed in tight. You will feel that your boat has slowed considerably, so you should bear off a little below where you ought to be pointing to get your boat going again. It often helps to *crack*, or slightly slack off your main, until the boat picks up speed. Then after way is on, she may be worked gently up to windward. Figure 33 explains the basic procedures in coming about.

It is not unusual for the beginner, when tacking for the first few times, to get himself into a frustrating and often embarrassing situation called being in stays or *in irons*. This usually occurs when a boat has insufficient way on when tacking. She will head up into the wind and then stop and drift helplessly backwards, taking much time to fall off to the point where her sails will fill again. Often when she does fall off, she will not even be on the tack her helmsman intended her to be on. To avoid this situation, be sure your boat has plenty of way before tacking, and do not put your helm down too fast. If you jam the tiller to leeward suddenly, the rudder will act as a brake and kill your boat's way. If you should find yourself in stays, the simplest way to recover is to *back* your jib, or pull in on its windward sheet so that it is trimmed up to windward, thus causing the wind to blow your bow off so that you may bear

FIGURE 32: FETCHING THE WINDWARD MARK

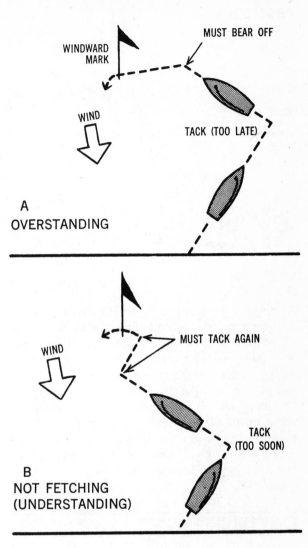

A
OVERSTANDING

B
NOT FETCHING (UNDERSTANDING)

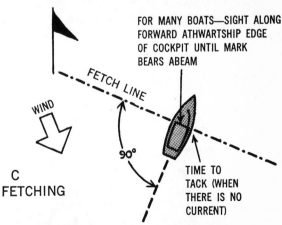

C
FETCHING

FETCH LINE (or LAY LINE)—A boat pointed at and fetching a mark is on her fetch line.
TO TAKE ADVANTAGE OF WIND SHIFTS, DO NOT SAIL UP TO FETCH LINE UNTIL FAIRLY CLOSE TO MARK.

35

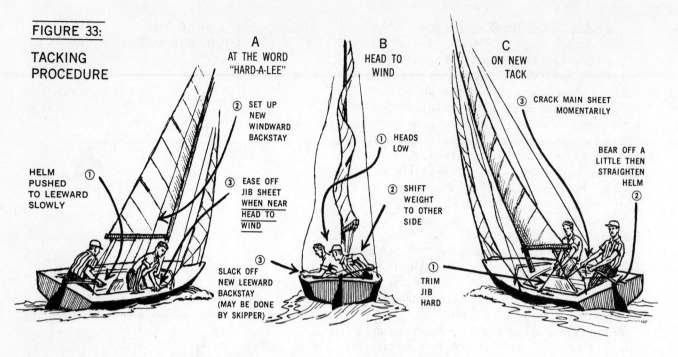

FIGURE 33:

TACKING PROCEDURE

A
AT THE WORD "HARD-A-LEE"

① HELM PUSHED TO LEEWARD SLOWLY

② SET UP NEW WINDWARD BACKSTAY

③ EASE OFF JIB SHEET WHEN NEAR HEAD TO WIND

③ SLACK OFF NEW LEEWARD BACKSTAY (MAY BE DONE BY SKIPPER)

B
HEAD TO WIND

① HEADS LOW

② SHIFT WEIGHT TO OTHER SIDE

① TRIM JIB HARD

C
ON NEW TACK

③ CRACK MAIN SHEET MOMENTARILY

② BEAR OFF A LITTLE THEN STRAIGHTEN HELM

off on the proper tack (see Figure 34). Should your boat not have a jib, trim in the main, and if she doesn't fall off on the correct tack, you must wait until she gathers *stern way* or drifts backwards, then reverse your helm or put your tiller over the same way you wish the bow to swing, as explained at the beginning of this section (see Figures 28 and 34). Backing the mainsail by pushing its boom up to windward will accelerate the backward movement, and also, if this sail is far enough forward, as on a cat boat, it will cause the bow to fall off in the opposite direction from the one in which it is backed (Figure 34).

DISTURBED WIND

Although this book will not go into racing tactics, which is a lengthy, involved subject not to be delved into by the novice until he has mastered the funda-

mentals, this book does lay the necessary basis for understanding racing and a few words about sailing in disturbed air are in order. A knowledge of this is of tremendous importance to the racing skipper, and it is well for the beginning sailor to start forming instinctive reactions to air that is turbulent. The two principal causes of wind disturbance have been mentioned in Section VI, "The Theory of Sailing." These causes are backwind and the wind shadow, or blanket. These might occur on other points of sailing, but I bring them up in this section on sailing to windward, because backwind, if present, is especially evident when sailing on the wind. One can easily notice this form of turbulence when the jib is trimmed in too flat or when the boat is following behind another which is close hauled.

As previously mentioned in the section on aerodynamics, backwind is a turbulent, swirling series of air eddies streaming from the leech of a sail. If headsails

FIGURE 34: IN STAYS

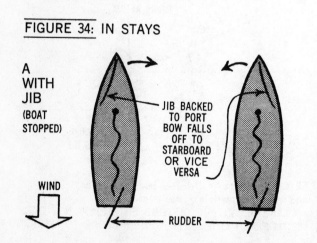

A
WITH JIB
(BOAT STOPPED)

WIND

JIB BACKED TO PORT BOW FALLS OFF TO STARBOARD OR VICE VERSA

RUDDER

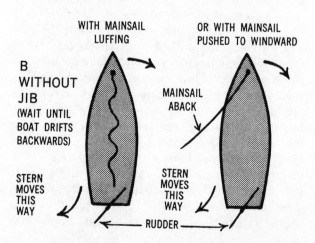

WITH MAINSAIL LUFFING

OR WITH MAINSAIL PUSHED TO WINDWARD

B
WITHOUT JIB
(WAIT UNTIL BOAT DRIFTS BACKWARDS)

MAINSAIL ABACK

STERN MOVES THIS WAY

STERN MOVES THIS WAY

RUDDER

are trimmed in too far they will pour these eddies into the lee side luffs of the after sails. As a matter of fact, not only the "degree" of trim is important in this matter but the "point" of trim, or the point from which the headsail is led, also has bearing on headsail backwind. There are actually two points to consider when determining the correct location for jib sheet leads, the fore and aft point and the athwartships point. The former usually lies slightly forward of the point where a projection of the jib's miter seam strikes the deck. If the sheet is led considerably forward of this point, the leech will be tight with the slot between main and jib narrow up aloft, while the jib's foot will curve out and be loose. In this case jib would back the upper part of the sail behind it. If, however, the jib is led abaft the miter projection, the reverse situation would be true. The jib's foot would be tight while its upper leech would fall off, and the main would be backed mostly near its foot (see Figure 35). The jib should be led so that the width of the slot is fairly uniform from top to bottom, and it should first begin to luff (shake at its luff when the boat is head up) at a point somewhat above the miter seam (as shown in Figure 35).

The athwartship point for the lead should be located approximately 12 degrees from the centerline of the boat (Figure 35) when the jib is a *lapper* (one that slightly overlaps the mast). Nonoverlapping jibs will have a wider angle, perhaps 15 degrees, and jibs with considerable overlap will use an angle of 8 degrees or slightly less. Ideal angles will vary with wind strength. In strong winds an outboard lead is usually best, but light winds call for a lead position that is farther inboard. Many boats are equipped with two lead positions, one near the rail and the other farther inboard, normally on the side deck.

When you are sailing in the vicinity of other boats, you must learn to be aware of backwind from their sails. If, when following another boat to windward, you find your boat performing erratically, you can almost be sure you are getting a dose of backwind from the leading vessel. Figure 36 shows the approximate area of backwind disturbance coming from a boat on the wind. The diagram shows the disturbed air coming from boat A. The shaded area between dotted lines represents the wind shadow from boat A. White boats 1, 2, and 3 have their wind clear or undisturbed with respect to boat A, while the black boats 1, 2, and 3 have their wind disturbed by A. Black boats 1 and 2 are in extremely bad positions because they are not only getting backwind, but black 1 is additionally slowed down by A's wake, and black 2 lies in A's wind shadow. Notice how far to windward A's backwind area extends to affect black 3. This is due to the deflection of the wind caused by the curvature of A's sails.

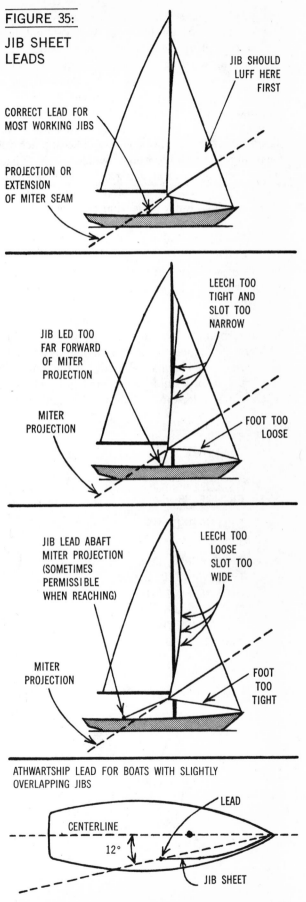

FIGURE 35:

JIB SHEET LEADS

JIB SHOULD LUFF HERE FIRST

CORRECT LEAD FOR MOST WORKING JIBS

PROJECTION OR EXTENSION OF MITER SEAM

LEECH TOO TIGHT AND SLOT TOO NARROW

JIB LED TOO FAR FORWARD OF MITER PROJECTION

MITER PROJECTION

FOOT TOO LOOSE

JIB LEAD ABAFT MITER PROJECTION (SOMETIMES PERMISSIBLE WHEN REACHING)

LEECH TOO LOOSE SLOT TOO WIDE

MITER PROJECTION

FOOT TOO TIGHT

ATHWARTSHIP LEAD FOR BOATS WITH SLIGHTLY OVERLAPPING JIBS

LEAD

CENTERLINE

12°

JIB SHEET

If you find yourself in any of these unfavorable positions as shown by the black boats, you should either tack or bear off below the leading boat's wind shadow to clear your wind. In the latter alternative, you might start or slack your sheets slightly for additional speed and try to gain enough momentum to carry you through the narrowest part of the wind shadow, then begin to work up to windward. A third alternative, if you were in black 3's position, would be to pinch your boat slightly and try to work to windward of A's backwind. *Splitting tacks* or going off on the other tack, however, is usually the simplest solution unless this carries you into unfavorable wind or current.

The wind shadow area, as Figure 36 shows, tapers to a point and extends about five mast lengths downwind from a boat. This zone is actually a lee, or an area where the wind has been partially blocked off. The wind shadow will be wider as the boat sails away from the wind until she is beam reaching, because she will be presenting her sails at a wider angle to the wind, thereby exposing a broader area to the wind. A sail may be blanketed not only by another sail but by any object which may block or partially cut off the wind. The beginning sailor should be prepared to be blanketed when sailing to leeward of lighthouses, high sea walls,

high shores, trees on shore, or large boats whether at anchor or under way. Sometimes this blanketing is so complete that a boat might be heeling over in a strong breeze with her crew on the windward side when she sails into a wind shadow, and suddenly her sails will lose their wind and cause the boat to right herself violently, almost making her crew fall over the windward side. If you see that you are about to be this thoroughly blanketed, alert your crew and tell them to move inboard. Don't bear off too far because you'll soon be through the wind shadow, and your new breeze might catch you headed too far off the wind and might suddenly heel you over.

HEADSAILS FOR WINDWARD SAILING

The *Genoa jib* has become more and more popular as the jib to carry windward in anything but a very strong breeze. As shown in Figure 37, it is a large jib with a long foot that overlaps the main considerably. It was first used by the Swedes in a race in 1927 at Genoa, hence its name. The Genoa jib is a very effective sail giving lots of drive by its great size and efficient slot. This sail nearly always trims from an adjustable lead on

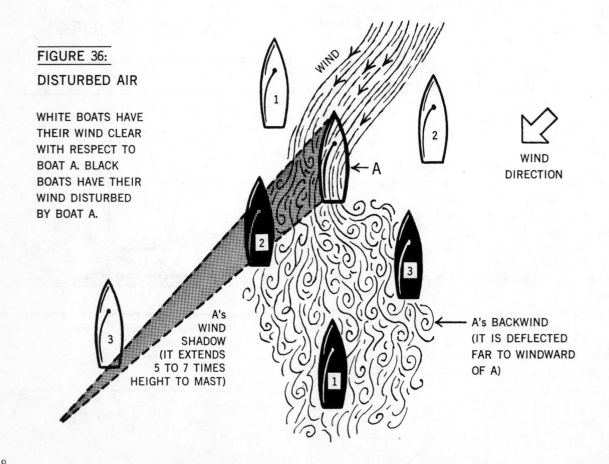

FIGURE 36:

DISTURBED AIR

WHITE BOATS HAVE THEIR WIND CLEAR WITH RESPECT TO BOAT A. BLACK BOATS HAVE THEIR WIND DISTURBED BY BOAT A.

WIND

A

WIND DIRECTION

A's WIND SHADOW (IT EXTENDS 5 TO 7 TIMES HEIGHT TO MAST)

A's BACKWIND (IT IS DEFLECTED FAR TO WINDWARD OF A)

FIGURE 37: HEADSAILS USED IN SAILING TO WINDWARD

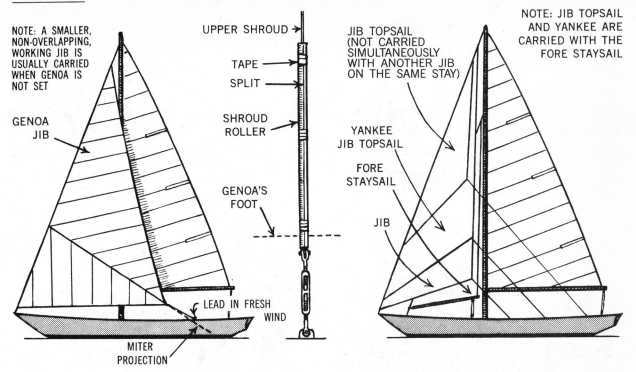

NOTE: A SMALLER, NON-OVERLAPPING, WORKING JIB IS USUALLY CARRIED WHEN GENOA IS NOT SET

GENOA JIB

UPPER SHROUD

TAPE

SPLIT

SHROUD ROLLER

GENOA'S FOOT

LEAD IN FRESH WIND

MITER PROJECTION

JIB TOPSAIL (NOT CARRIED SIMULTANEOUSLY WITH ANOTHER JIB ON THE SAME STAY)

NOTE: JIB TOPSAIL AND YANKEE ARE CARRIED WITH THE FORE STAYSAIL

YANKEE JIB TOPSAIL

FORE STAYSAIL

JIB

Avoid taking genoa sheet from lead block directly to winch (as shown by dotted arrow). This puts extra strain on genoa track. Use a strong turning block bolted to deck to reduce strain on track.

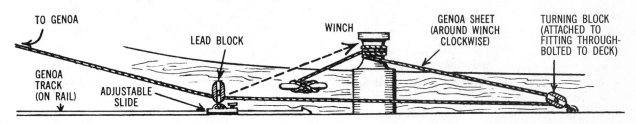

TO GENOA

LEAD BLOCK

WINCH

GENOA SHEET (AROUND WINCH CLOCKWISE)

TURNING BLOCK (ATTACHED TO FITTING THROUGH-BOLTED TO DECK)

GENOA TRACK (ON RAIL)

ADJUSTABLE SLIDE

a slide which runs on a track attached to the rail or just inboard of the rail (see Figure 37). The Genoa, or *Jenny* as it is sometimes called, also trims outside of the shrouds or side stays. The lead should not be adjusted so that the sail is pressed against the end of the spreaders, nor should it lead so that its foot is stretched excessively against the shrouds. Usually the sail is trimmed correctly for beating in moderate winds when its upper leech is just a few inches or so away from the spreaders and its foot lies easy against the shrouds. In light airs it often helps the Jenny's shape to lead it slightly farther forward, particularly so if you are not absolutely close hauled, but are reaching. It is very important to tape or wrap in felt the tips of the spreaders where they touch the jib to prevent chafe. A reinforcing patch on the sail at this spot is a good idea. You should also watch for the chafe where the jib lies against the shrouds. Many skippers put rollers on the most outboard shrouds.

Rollers are usually narrow, split, hollow tubes of either rubber, plastic, or wood which are put on around the stay and wrapped with tape or tied so that the split will stay closed (see Figure 37).

Cutters normally have a double-head rig or carry two headsails, a fore staysail with a jib topsail or yankee jib (see Figure 37).

Working jibs and fore staysails are often fitted with booms so that the jib sheet may be led to a traveler. This arrangement eliminates the necessity of double jib sheets. The boat may be tacked without releasing one sheet and taking in on the other. The lead merely slides from one end of the traveler to the other, and the single sheet may be left cleated (see Figure 38). This arrangement is obviously for ease of handling when one is short-handed or leisurely cruising.

When sailing to windward with a large overlapping headsail such as a Genoa, one can expect a little more

FIGURE 38: A SELF-ATTENDING JIB

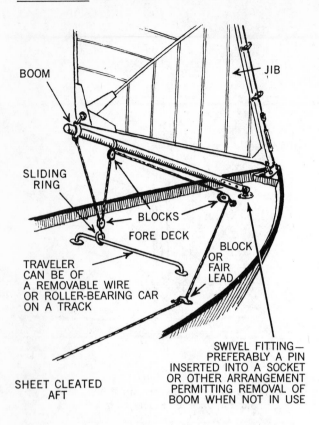

BOOM

JIB

SLIDING RING

BLOCKS

FORE DECK

BLOCK OR FAIR LEAD

TRAVELER CAN BE OF A REMOVABLE WIRE OR ROLLER-BEARING CAR ON A TRACK

SHEET CLEATED AFT

SWIVEL FITTING— PREFERABLY A PIN INSERTED INTO A SOCKET OR OTHER ARRANGEMENT PERMITTING REMOVAL OF BOOM WHEN NOT IN USE

FIGURE 39: AIDS TO HELMSMANSHIP THROUGH THE SENSES

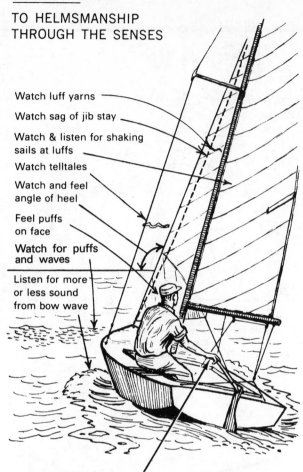

Watch luff yarns

Watch sag of jib stay

Watch & listen for shaking sails at luffs

Watch telltales

Watch and feel angle of heel

Feel puffs on face

Watch for puffs and waves

Listen for more or less sound from bow wave

FEEL BALANCE OF HELM (WEATHER OR LEE HELM). IN LIGHT AIRS USE ONLY TWO FINGERS ON TILLER OF SMALL BOAT.

backwind than normal, especially in a good breeze. For this reason many skippers purposely carry a slight luff in their mainsail under these conditions. When sailing in this manner, many helmsmen prefer to sit to leeward where they can watch and sail by the luff on the jib instead of the mainsail. From this position the helmsman can still see the windward telltale, but he can also see when the luff on his jib starts to *break* or first begins to flap, and he can bear off slightly to keep his boat moving. However, if there is a good breeze, the helmsman should put his weight to windward to help right the boat, particularly if she is small. A small racer usually has a tiller extension, as described in Section III, to allow the helmsman to hike out as far as possible. From this position he can easily watch the mainsail luff and look at the water to windward for puffs and occasional choppy waves that might need to be dodged. Of course he may also watch the telltale and masthead fly from the windward side and if he moves as far forward as possible, he can see the extreme forward edge of the jib luff and headstay. When the headstay sags off, the helmsman knows that he is full and by, but when it is almost perfectly straight, he is perhaps pointing a little too high. This is explained in Figure 39. The dotted sag line in the diagram is slightly exaggerated for clar-

ity. The headstay should never be that loose. In fact, the tighter it is, the better—although there will always be at least a little sag. This method works best when the water is not too rough, because in a seaway the mast will jump around somewhat, causing the stay to move. Sailing in rough seas is an art in itself and will be discussed in Section XI.

Luff telltales are another aid to helmsmanship. These are usually wool or acrylic yarns taped to the jib on both sides or threaded through the sail about 5 percent of the *chord* (straight line distance from luff to leach) abaft the luff at about a third of the luff's length up from the tack. The sail cloth is normally transparent enough to see the yarn on the leeward side as well as the windward side of the sail. One should try to sail so that the yarns are streaming directly aft rather than fluttering wildly or twirling around. If the windward yarn twirls, bear off, but if the leeward yarn twirls, head up a bit. Sometimes strong sunlight on the sail will destroy its transparency, and for this condition a telltale window is needed. A typical window of Mylar is shown in Figure A.   Many sailors prefer that the telltales be black yarn for best visibility, but others prefer that the yarns be red on the port side and green on the starboard side (see Figure B).

LUFF TELLTALES

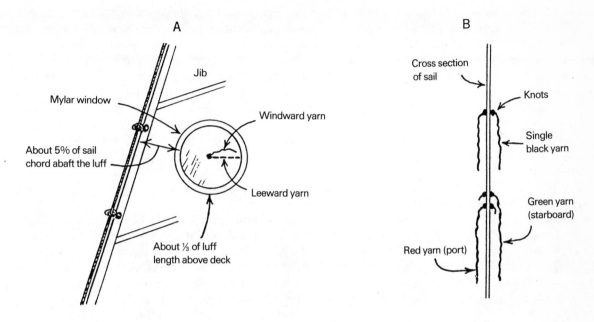

A

Jib

Mylar window

Windward yarn

About 5% of sail chord abaft the luff

Leeward yarn

About ⅓ of luff length above deck

B

Cross section of sail

Knots

Single black yarn

Green yarn (starboard)

Red yarn (port)

SAILING OFF THE WIND

In the previous section we discussed sailing a boat to windward. The coming section will deal with sailing off the wind or to leeward. Although some sailors think of the expression "off the wind" as meaning to run or sail before the wind, I intend the expression to mean any point of sailing except beating to windward. This, of course, would include reaching as well as running.

REACHING

General sail positions for off-wind sailing have been discussed in Section VI; however, let us review them briefly. In bearing off from being close hauled, we slack sheets slightly when close reaching, start them farther (about halfway out) when beam reaching, still farther when broad reaching, and slack them all the way (without the boom touching the shroud) when running. Then if we are moving particularly fast, the sails are trimmed a little flatter due to the apparent wind coming from farther ahead.

There is a very simple method of determining the approximate correct sail trim when reaching. First the boat is put on her proper course, then the sheets are slacked off until the sails begin to shake at their luffs,

and finally the sheets are pulled in until this luffing or shaking discontinues. Care should be taken to see that sheets are not trimmed too flat when reaching. For the jib especially, a good aid to proper trim is the luff telltales discussed at the end of the previous section. When the leeward yarns are twirling, this indicates that the jib is trimmed too flat, resulting in its being *stalled*, suffering loss of lift as a result of the flow becoming detached from the sail. Overtrimming not only causes loss of thrust or drive from stalling but also from the misdirection of thrust away from the boat's heading and from excessive heeling when it is blowing hard.

In light airs, sheets should be eased slightly to get maximum draft in the sails, but in moderate airs, sails should be trimmed a bit flatter. Once the sails are properly trimmed for reaching, they should not merely be left in that position, because breezes are variable. The experienced racing skipper will play or constantly adjust his sheets. He will continually experiment to see if the sails might be slacked off just a little more without their luffs beginning to shake. When reaching, some skippers carry a special jib called the *reaching jib*, *balloon jib*, or *drifter* (Figure 40). This jib is usually

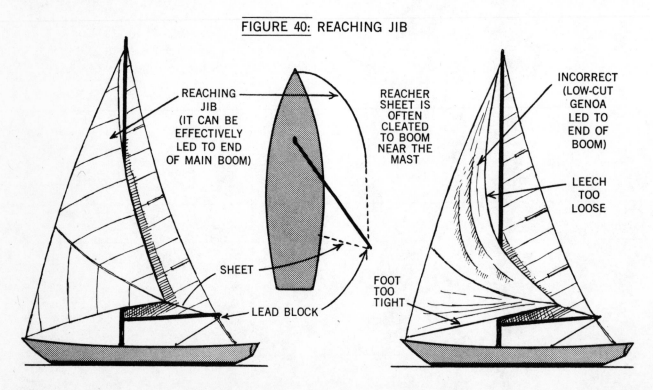

FIGURE 40: REACHING JIB

REACHING JIB (IT CAN BE EFFECTIVELY LED TO END OF MAIN BOOM)

SHEET

LEAD BLOCK

REACHER SHEET IS OFTEN CLEATED TO BOOM NEAR THE MAST

FOOT TOO TIGHT

INCORRECT (LOW-CUT GENOA LED TO END OF BOOM)

LEECH TOO LOOSE

carried in light to medium winds, particularly when racing. It is made of light material and cut high in the foot, with its clew high off the deck. One of the main reasons for this high clew is to prevent excessive twist and permit the jib to be led from a block attached to the end of the main boom (see the diagram). This lead is beneficial on a reach when sheets are slacked, because the jib is led the maximum distance outboard where it is more efficient and throws less backwind against the main. Genoas are usually cut too low in the foot with their clews too close to the deck to be led from the end of the main boom. When this is done the jib's foot becomes too tight while its leech aloft becomes too loose and falls way off, as shown in Figure 40.

Aside from the reaching jib there are other *light sails*, made of light material, used primarily for racing, which are helpful in reaching. The most common of these are illustrated in Figure 41. The mizzen staysail is set between the mizzen and the mainmast on a yawl or ketch. It sheets from the end of the mizzen boom. This sail usually cannot be carried effectively when sailing closer to the wind than a beam reach. The *gollywobbler*, more properly though less commonly called the *main topmast balloon staysail*, is carried on staysail schooners. It covers the area between the foremast and mainmast, though some even extend beyond the foremast to cover the fore triangle. This sail, like the reaching jib, usually trims off the end of the main boom. The *spinnaker staysail* may be set on any boat that carries a spinnaker (provided class rules allow it to be carried when racing). The spinnaker itself will be dealt with later in this section. The spinnaker staysail, as shown in the diagram, is a balloon-like staysail which is set abaft and beneath the spinnaker. Although they are often carried when running, none of these reaching staysails are as efficient when carried directly before the wind because they are partially blanketed by the sail behind them. The mizzen staysail is sometimes effectively carried on a running yawl when her mizzen is lowered. On a modern yawl the mizzen is small, but it is large enough to blanket the mizzen staysails when the wind is dead aft, so it often pays to take the mizzen off and carry the larger, fuller mizzen staysail.

THE BOOM VANG

Figure 42 illustrates a device used to control the mainsail's shape which is especially effective when sailing downwind. This is called the *boom vang* or *kicking strap*, and it is becoming more and more popular. Most of today's racing skippers would feel that their boats were undressed without a boom vang. The device is particularly important on small planing boats, but it is

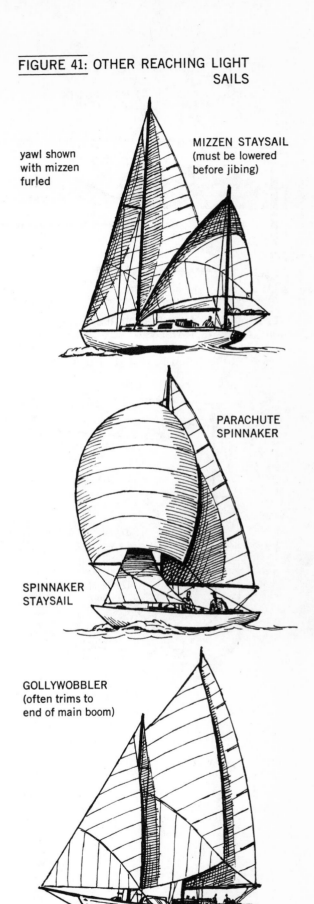

FIGURE 41: OTHER REACHING LIGHT SAILS

yawl shown with mizzen furled

MIZZEN STAYSAIL (must be lowered before jibing)

PARACHUTE SPINNAKER

SPINNAKER STAYSAIL

GOLLYWOBBLER (often trims to end of main boom)

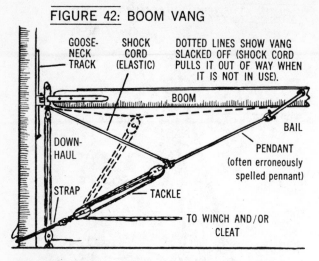

FIGURE 42: BOOM VANG

GOOSE-NECK TRACK

SHOCK CORD (ELASTIC)

DOTTED LINES SHOW VANG SLACKED OFF (SHOCK CORD PULLS IT OUT OF WAY WHEN IT IS NOT IN USE).

BOOM

DOWN-HAUL

BAIL

PENDANT (often erroneously spelled pennant)

STRAP

TACKLE

TO WINCH AND/OR CLEAT

NOTE: THIS TYPE OF VANG REQUIRES A VERY STRONG GOOSENECK WHOSE TRACK SHOULD BE BOLTED TO MAST. BOATS WITH LIGHT ALUMINUM BOOMS REQUIRE GREATER USE OF THE VANG.

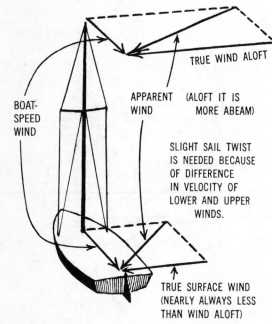

TRUE WIND ALOFT

APPARENT WIND

(ALOFT IT IS MORE ABEAM)

BOAT-SPEED WIND

SLIGHT SAIL TWIST IS NEEDED BECAUSE OF DIFFERENCE IN VELOCITY OF LOWER AND UPPER WINDS.

TRUE SURFACE WIND (NEARLY ALWAYS LESS THAN WIND ALOFT)

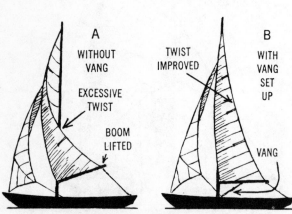

A

WITHOUT VANG

TWIST IMPROVED

B

WITH VANG SET UP

EXCESSIVE TWIST

BOOM LIFTED

VANG

used on nearly all racers, even on boats as large as those that compete for the *America's Cup**. As shown in the diagram, the vang, which is attached to the boom, consists of a short wire called a pendant which supports a *tackle,* or a pulling system of ropes and blocks. This is designed to pull the boom down. The pendant's point of attachment to the boom is usually about one-third of the boom's length from the mast, while the tackle's lower point of attachment is usually around the mast near the deck, if the boat is decked over, but near the mast step or around the base of the mast if the boat is open (undecked).

The purpose of the boom vang is also illustrated in Figure 42, which compares two boats: A without a vang on her main boom, and B with a vang. Notice that A's boom is lifted and the leech of her sail curves to such an extent that the sail aloft is in a position for running while the sail's foot is in a position for beam reaching. In other words the sail has an extreme twist, and much of its effectiveness is lost. Boat B, however, with the vang, has the head and foot of her mainsail more nearly in the same plane. This is because her boom is being pulled down by the vang. Some twist in a sail is desirable because there is more wind aloft, which causes the apparent wind aloft to be farther abeam (see Figure 42), but an average main with a light boom and no vang has far too much twist. In good breezes the vang should be set up much tighter than in light airs, for it will have a tendency to flatten the mainsail and tighten the jib stay. For these reasons the vang is often carried to windward in a breeze in which the skipper wants his jib luff tight and his main a little flatter, without much draft or curvature. In extremely light airs many skippers do not use the vang at all because they prefer a maximum of draft even if their sail is twisted.

RUNNING

Many experienced sailors think that getting the best performance from a boat when running before the wind requires as much skill as beating to windward, because a boat should be worked downwind in much the same way that she is worked to windward. The procedure used when going upwind, however, is just the opposite of that used for running. I'll explain why. Let us recall what we learned about working a boat to windward in an unsteady breeze. When a puff strikes her sails she begins to heel, so the helmsman points her closer to the wind in order to stop excessive heeling and to make the maximum distance to windward. In the lulls he does just the opposite. He bears off so that the

America's Cup—A trophy won by the yacht *America* from the British in 1851 and periodically competed for in a series of sailing races between an American yacht and a foreign yacht.

44

boat will pick up speed. When she is moving her best, the helmsman may again parry the puffs to see how high he can point yet still keep his boat moving.

When running, however, it is the other way around. The helmsman bears off in the puffs and heads up in the lulls. This procedure is shown in Figure 43. The boat in this diagram is running for a downwind mark. She starts directly for the mark, but the wind dies slightly and she slows down. Her skipper heads up a little and trims his sheets slightly so that he is almost broad reaching because he knows that reaching is the faster point of sailing; also his jib will not be blanketed by the main, and in general his sails will draw better. His boat then picks up speed, but she is no longer headed for the mark. The skipper realizes that he must work his boat more to leeward. At this moment his boat is struck by a puff, and she begins to heel. This is a good opportunity for the helmsman to bear off because the boat will have sufficient power from the puff to retain her speed, and when she has the wind dead aft, her heeling will be minimized. The procedure is repeated until the mark is reached. Excessive heeling to leeward when running will give most boats a strong weather helm, and of course this slows a boat down because of the rudder's drag as it is held over to prevent the boat from heading up. Many racing skippers, in fact, prefer to have their boats heeled slightly to windward when running to prevent this weather helm.

A common practice used when racing for a leeward mark is *tacking downwind*. This is shown in Figure 44. Here the skipper broad reaches his boat in one direction then jibes and goes off in the other direction, making a zigzag course toward the leeward mark. The theory of this strategy is that a boat tacking downwind will make so much more speed when broad reaching than when running that the extra distance she has to travel will be more than compensated for. In other words a straight line is the shortest distance between two points, but not necessarily the fastest one to follow! This strategy, however, should not be overdone.

When sailing before the wind in a centerboard boat, it is best to pull the board up most or all of the way because on this point of sailing, lateral resistance is not needed and a deep board merely produces speed-retarding drag. Most skippers, however, prefer not to carry the board all the way up in a hard breeze, because if it is down a little, the board will add to the boat's stability and will help keep her from rolling and yawning in a following sea. Yawning is the tendency of a boat to swing from side to side as the following seas roll under her stern or quarter. In an extremely heavy sea where a boat is yawning severely, there may be some danger of her *broaching to*—swinging around to such an extent that the boat lies broadside to the wind and waves. Broaching to is usually caused by a vessel's

FIGURE 43: WORKING TO LEEWARD

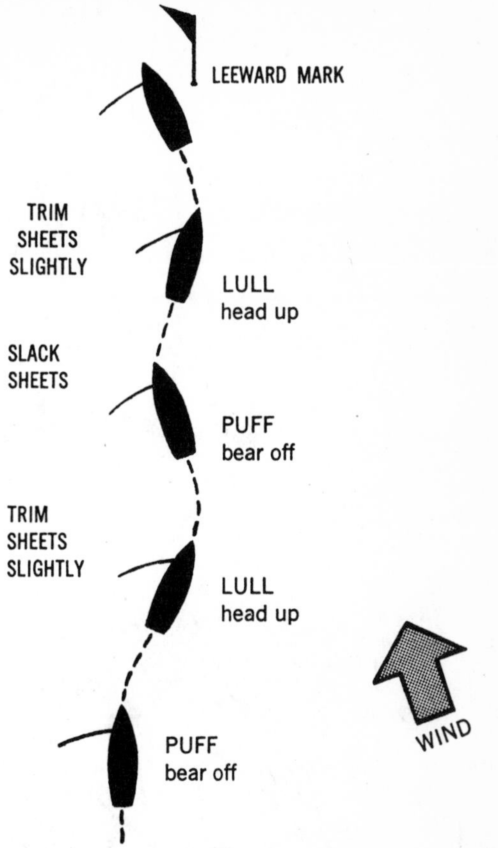

LEEWARD MARK

TRIM SHEETS SLIGHTLY

LULL head up

SLACK SHEETS

PUFF bear off

TRIM SHEETS SLIGHTLY

LULL head up

WIND

PUFF bear off

FIGURE 44: TACKING DOWNWIND

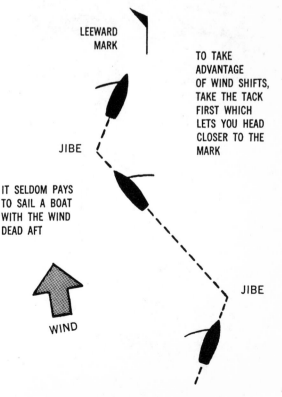

LEEWARD MARK

TO TAKE ADVANTAGE OF WIND SHIFTS, TAKE THE TACK FIRST WHICH LETS YOU HEAD CLOSER TO THE MARK

JIBE

IT SELDOM PAYS TO SAIL A BOAT WITH THE WIND DEAD AFT

WIND

JIBE

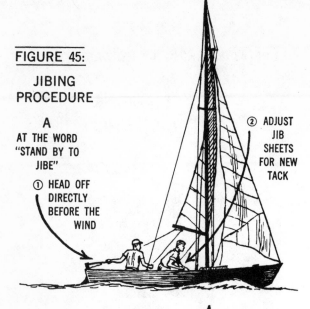

FIGURE 45:

JIBING PROCEDURE

A
AT THE WORD "STAND BY TO JIBE"

① HEAD OFF DIRECTLY BEFORE THE WIND

② ADJUST JIB SHEETS FOR NEW TACK

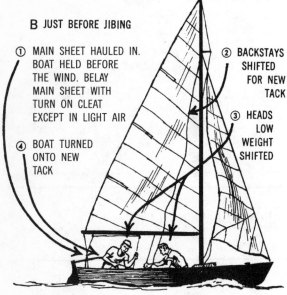

B JUST BEFORE JIBING

① MAIN SHEET HAULED IN. BOAT HELD BEFORE THE WIND. BELAY MAIN SHEET WITH TURN ON CLEAT EXCEPT IN LIGHT AIR

④ BOAT TURNED ONTO NEW TACK

② BACKSTAYS SHIFTED FOR NEW TACK

③ HEADS LOW WEIGHT SHIFTED

C AT THE WORD "JIBE-HO" BOOM SWINGS ACROSS (Jibe completed from starboard to port tack)

① STRAIGHTEN HELM. SLACK MAIN SHEET QUICKLY. THEN STEER ONTO NEW COURSE

② TRIM JIB FOR NEW COURSE

burying her bow in the water as a wave lifts her stern. This can rarely happen to a well-designed boat except in heavy weather. However, if a sailor should be in conditions that cause his boat to yaw severely with a tendency to broach to, he should reduce her sail to slow the boat. The proper procedure for doing this is to lower or shorten the aftermost sail first when running before the wind. On a yawl or ketch this would mean the mizzen, while on a sloop, cutter, or schooner it would be the mainsail. (Reefing and reducing sail will be discussed in Section XI.) Trimming the jib or staysail in flat will also help prevent broaching to. When sailing under these conditions the skipper and crew should move fairly far aft so that the bow will lift instead of burying in the seas. This weight aft will also help keep the rudder completely submerged for maximum steering control.

JIBING

The reader will recall that jibing is a turning maneuver in which a vessel is put from one tack to the other by turning downwind. The jibe occurs when a vessel, sailing dead before the wind, is turned to leeward. Her sails begin to fill from their foreside, and the wind suddenly forces them to swing across the boat (Figure 22).

Many beginning sailors seem to have a fear of jibing, probably because they have heard of mishaps connected with the maneuver. However, while a jibe should be treated with respect, there is nothing to fear when it is properly executed and done intentionally. Most mishaps connected with this kind of turn are the result of an unintentional or accidental jibe.

First let's see how a boat should be properly jibed, and then we will look at the chief reasons for accidental jibes so that we can learn how to avoid them. Figure 45 shows the step-by-step jibing procedure for a small sloop. The skipper must first alert the crew to his intention with the warning, "Stand by to jibe." Then he puts his boat before the wind if he is not already running, while his crew shifts the jib sheets, casting off the one that is cleated, and cleating the one that is not made fast. The mainsail is hauled in amidships either by the skipper or a crew member. If the boat has running backstays, these must be changed so that the boom won't strike the leeward backstay after swinging across. The skipper then gives the warning, "Jibe-ho," which means that he is jibing at that moment. He and the crew immediately duck their heads and shift their weight to the new windward side while the boat is steered slightly and gradually to leeward. As soon as the boom swings over and the sail fills on the other side, the helmsman will feel the boat develop a slight tendency to head up into the wind on this new tack. The helm should therefore be momentarily reversed, then straightened up so that the boat will stay before the wind but on the new tack. Then the main sheet is slacked off to its correct position for the boat's new course.

Accidental jibes are usually caused by inattentiveness on the part of the helmsman. If he is sailing *by the lee*, or dead before the wind, so that the boat is on the verge of jibing, he must be alert every second because a slight shift of wind or a sea rolling under the stern could make him jibe unintentionally. He must keep his gaze on the mainsail to watch for the first sign of its backing or beginning to fill from the fore side. When this happens, he would instantly head the boat up a little toward the wind to make the sails fill on their proper side. A jib can warn the helmsman that he is sailing by the lee because it nearly always swings over or jibes before the main. It is always safer to sail a boat not dead before the wind but with the wind a little more on the quarter, particularly when there is a following sea which might make the boat yaw. If it is necessary to sail by the lee in a following sea, a *preventer* should be rigged. This is simply a lashing on the main boom that is made fast to some secure point forward of the boom to hold it forward in case of an unintentional jibe.

On most modern boats, the chief dangers in an accidental jibe are that someone might get hit on the head, knocked overboard, or that a sheet might become fouled around the tiller or even someone's neck. On boats of older design, there were other dangers. Formerly, sails and spars were longer and heavier, and a *flying jibe*, or one made without pulling in the main sheet to ease the boom across, could put a severe strain on the rigging.

Whoever handles the main sheet should take a turn around the cleat when jibing in a breeze, so that the sheet will not run too rapidly through his hands as the boom slams across. Jibing a gaff-rigged boat in a strong breeze can involve the risk of a *goose wing*. This occurs when the boom and foot of the mainsail swing across onto the new tack while the gaff and head of the sail do not swing but remain on the original tack (see Figure 46). The proper procedure for getting out of this predicament is to jibe back onto the original tack and then try jibing again. This time the main sheet should be pulled in as far as it can possibly come to prevent the mainsail from twisting before it jibes onto the new tack. The goose wing rarely happens on a Marconi-rigged boat, especially when the sheet is pulled in adequately before jibing.

The racing skipper sometimes uses a semi-flying jibe (with the sheets pulled only partway in) when rounding a mark so that he may turn in the quickest possible time, but the jibe is intentional and always under con-trol. His sheets are clear so as not to foul, and he and his crew are ready instantly to shift their weights to the new windward side. In this kind of jibe, the boom vang is usually set up tight if it is the kind that is secured at the mast's base as illustrated in Figure 42. This helps hold the boom down so that it can't goose-wing. Some boom vangs are secured off center on the side deck or rail, and obviously these types must be released before jibing.

THE SPINNAKER

The spinnaker is such an effective sail for downwind sailing that a boat without one cannot even hope to race against a boat that is carrying one of these balloon-like sails. The first spinnaker is said to have been flown well over a hundred years ago by a British yacht named *Sphinx*, and the sail was referred to as the "Sphinxer," or "Sphinx's acre." This is supposedly how the sail got its name. The early spinnaker, however, was different from its modern descendant. The former was called the *single luff* or *flat spinnaker* and it had little more than half the girth of the contemporary version,

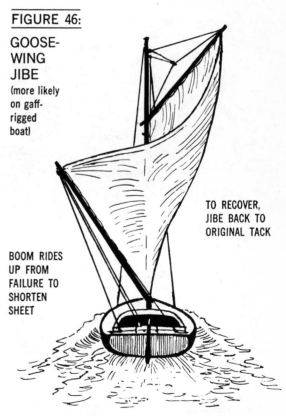

FIGURE 46:

GOOSE-WING JIBE
(more likely on gaff-rigged boat)

TO RECOVER, JIBE BACK TO ORIGINAL TACK

BOOM RIDES UP FROM FAILURE TO SHORTEN SHEET

NOTE: IF ROLLING SEVERELY WHILE RUNNING, A BOAT WITH LOW FREEBOARD AND LONG BOOM MIGHT NEED HER BOOM'S END SLIGHTLY LIFTED WITH TOPPING LIFT TO PREVENT DIPPING BOOM IN WATER. THIS MAY INCREASE TENDENCY TO GOOSE-WING.

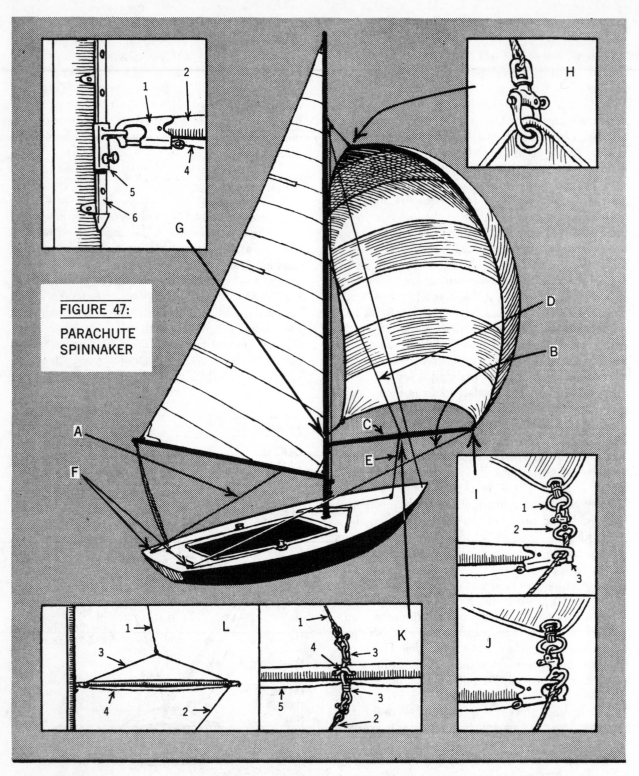

FIGURE 47:

PARACHUTE SPINNAKER

A   SPINNAKER SHEET

B   GUY (sheet & guy
    lead outside shrouds)

C   SPINNAKER POLE

D   POLE LIFT

E   POLE DOWNHAUL (foreguy)

F   SHEET & GUY

    LEAD BLOCKS

G   POLE FITTING & SLIDE
    (1) pole fitting (at each
        end of pole)
    (2) pole (3) spring-loaded pin
    (4) lanyard (pull to open pin)
    (5) adjustable slide
    (6) track (on mast's fore side)

H   SPINNAKER HALYARD SWIVEL
    SHACKLE (sometimes at each
    end of halyard—often a swivel
    is permanently attached
    to spinnaker head)

I   SPINNAKER TACK
    (1) metal ring lashed to
        tack grommet (optional)
    (2) Swivel ring shackle
        (same arrangement
        at clew)
    (3) pole snapped on guy

J   ALTERNATE METHOD
    (pole snapped to ring
    on shackle—usually not
    recommended except to
    avoid chafe)

K   MIDDLE OF POLE
    (1) lift (2) downhaul
    (3) wire or rope strop
    (4) eye strap
    (5) continuous lanyard

L   ALTERNATE METHOD
    (1) lift (2) downhaul (may
    be attached to a bridle under
    the boom)
    (3) bridle (4) lanyard

which is called the *parachute spinnaker*. The older type was quite effective, for it was often used in conjunction with a balloon jib and rigged so that the spinnaker would spill its air into the jib. However, this arrangement could not compare with the power and drive of the modern parachute.

The beginning sailor should thoroughly master the fundamentals of running and jibing before attempting to set a spinnaker, for this sail can be complicated to handle. Figure 47 illustrates the parachute spinnaker with its principal lines and fittings. To simplify matters, all lines and rigging which are not directly related to the spinnaker have been left off the diagram.

As you can see, the spinnaker has the shape of a balloon-like, spherical triangle and is held out on the side opposite the mainsail by a pole. The sail is held in place at its three corners only: at its head by a halyard, at its tack by the pole with a *guy*, and at its clew by a sheet. The guy controls the fore and aft position of the pole, pulling it back until it is almost at right angles to the boat's heading or allowing it to go forward until it swings against the headstay, at which position it is almost parallel to the boat's heading. When running, the pole is pulled aft until it nearly touches the forward shroud, but when reaching, it is guyed forward. The spinnaker usually cannot be carried with great effectiveness when the true wind is coming forward of the beam. In other words, a boat with the average spinnaker can rarely point effectively much higher than a beam reach. At this point, the sail is guyed all the way forward. A good rule to remember is that the fore and

aft position of the pole should always be approximately at right angles to the apparent wind. Correct spinnaker pole positions for running, broad reaching, and beam reaching are shown in Figure 48. For clarity guys and sheets in the drawings are represented by dotted lines.

Except in very light airs the spinnaker's foot should be lifted to give the sail more belly. The harder the breeze, the more it should be lifted. This is done by lifting the spinnaker pole. The pole may be raised at either end because, as Figure 47 shows, the inboard end of the pole is secured to the mast at an adjustable slide on a track while the pole's outboard end may be raised by the *pole lift*. Figure 49 shows a spinnaker pole lifted at three different positions. Although the spinnaker is lifted the most in A, this position is nearly always incorrect because it brings the sail too close to the mast. Position C, where the pole is perfectly horizontal, is preferred by many experts because the sail is held a maximum distance from the mast; however, some authorities like position B because in addition to the sail having more lift, the guy follows the same line of direction as the pole, making the same angle to the mast, and this puts less strain on the pole when sailing in a breeze.

The spinnaker downhaul, often called the *foreguy*, pulls the pole down, preventing it from riding up. Sometimes this line is rigged from the outboard end of the pole instead of from its middle. If the downhaul is rigged from the pole's end, the lift should also be rigged from the end or middle of a *bridle* or wire span attached to each end of the pole, as shown in Figure 47,

FIGURE 48: FORE & AFT SPINNAKER POLE POSITIONS

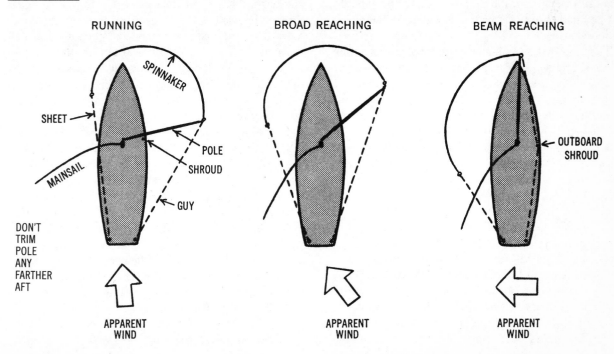

RUNNING   BROAD REACHING   BEAM REACHING

49

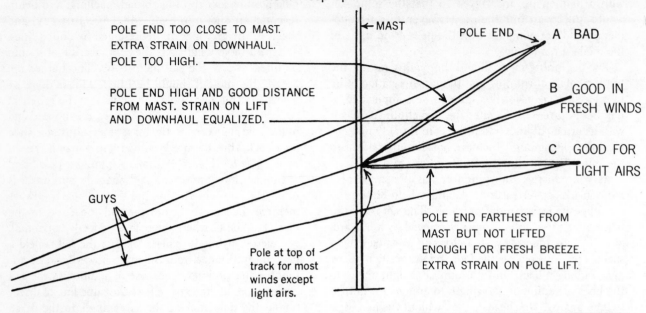

FIGURE 49: POLE LIFT ADJUSTMENTS (Tack should not be lifted above height of clew. Keep spinnaker's foot horizontal.)

POLE END TOO CLOSE TO MAST. EXTRA STRAIN ON DOWNHAUL. POLE TOO HIGH.

POLE END HIGH AND GOOD DISTANCE FROM MAST. STRAIN ON LIFT AND DOWNHAUL EQUALIZED.

← MAST

POLE END → A BAD

B GOOD IN FRESH WINDS

C GOOD FOR LIGHT AIRS

GUYS

POLE END FARTHEST FROM MAST BUT NOT LIFTED ENOUGH FOR FRESH BREEZE. EXTRA STRAIN ON POLE LIFT.

Pole at top of track for most winds except light airs.

so that the downward pull is directly under the upward pull. Quite often there is another bridle under the boom, which accepts the downhaul.

The spinnaker sheet should be led almost as far aft as possible when the boat has a wide stern. Occasionally it is led through a block on the end of the main boom, as with a reaching jib. The spinnaker's clew (controlled by the sheet) should be the same level as its tack (attached at the pole). In other words, the tack and clew should be the same height above the deck. If the wind is not sufficient to lift the clew up high, the pole should not be lifted excessively high or it will cause the sail to be lopsided.

There are two principal ways to set a spinnaker: by stopping and with the *turtle*. Except on a large boat or in a heavy breeze, I prefer the latter method because it is simpler and often quicker. The turtle is a container which holds the bundled spinnaker on the deck before it is hoisted. Although the first turtle was made of plywood and rubber, most are made from cloth today. Often an ordinary sailbag serves the purpose. A simple variation of the turtle is shown in Figure 50. This is essentially a cloth bag secured to a piece of plywood which holds the spinnaker to the deck just forward of the headstay (the plywood is not needed if the boat has a bow pulpit to which the bag can be lashed). This turtle's open end has a drawstring of shock cord (elastic cord) to temporarily hold in the sail's three corners, which are peeking out of the bag. These corners are rigged to their proper lines, and the pole's forward end is usually snapped onto the guy as shown in the diagram. The pole's after end is already hooked to the

mast track slide. The secret of setting a spinnaker is to have everything properly set up in advance. The spinnaker halyard block is above the headstay or jibstay so the end of the halyard which fastens to the spinnaker's head should be to leeward of the stay. It is always wise to take a careful look aloft to see that everything is clear before hoisting.

The other method of setting a spinnaker is shown in Figure 51. This consists of bundling the sail between its leeches or edges, being careful that it is not twisted, and tying it with short stops of weak cotton or string or thread. The sail is then rigged to its sheet, guy, and halyard and hoisted while stopped. When it is up, and the pole is guyed to its proper position, the sheet is given a hard yank which breaks the lower stops above the legs, the bundled-up, lower corners (see Figure 51). With the lower stops broken, the spinnaker's foot will billow out in the breeze and this should exert sufficient force against the upper stops to break them. Sometimes in light airs, however, it takes considerable tugging and yanking on the sheet to break the stops. Under these conditions, I think it is better to use the turtle.

Once the spinnaker is set, one of two techniques or a combination of the two may be used to sail the boat. We have seen that the wind is frequently variable; so with one technique, the boat is set on a steady course and the spinnaker is adjusted for every shift of wind. In the second method, the spinnaker is left in one position of trim and the boat's course is altered to correspond with the wind shifts.

In the first method, spinnaker trim is adjusted with the sheet and guy. If the wind shifts so that it is coming from farther aft, the sheet is slacked off and the pole is guyed farther aft. The reverse is done if the wind shifts forward. Actually, the first adjustment should be made with the sheet because it may be found that the shift is only momentary. If, after the sheet has been adjusted, the shifted wind looks as though it will hold from its new direction for a little while at least, then the guy should be adjusted.

The second method of sailing with the spinnaker requires an alert helmsman. He must keep his eyes glued on the sail for the first sign of its breaking or beginning to collapse. When it starts to break, it will bulge from the forward side, and the helmsman must immediately change course. Often it is difficult to tell which way to turn, because the spinnaker's break might be caused by being too far off the wind, sailing by the lee, in which case it might be blanketed by the mainsail; or the break might be caused by the spinnaker's luffing from sailing too high. Careful observation will usually tell the difference. A blanketed spinnaker will begin shakingly to collapse all over, while a luffing spinnaker will curl or bulge inward at its luff or windward edge. If the helmsman cannot immediately determine whether he is sailing too high or too low, he should consult his masthead fly or telltales and remember that the spinnaker should be at right angles to the apparent wind (see Figure 52). The masthead flies indicating the apparent wind are shown as heavy arrows in the boats' centers. In A the fly shows the wind to be coming from dead aft and the angle between fly and pole to be acute (less than a right angle), so the helmsman should head up a little. In B the fly indicates the wind is more on the beam, with the angle between pole and fly obtuse (more than a right angle), so the helmsman should bear off a little.

Even if a boat is being sailed by the second (change course for wind) method, it is wise to have a man stand by the sheet, for if the spinnaker luffs badly, a complete collapse can often be averted by giving the sheet a quick tug. This will momentarily fill the sail while the helmsman changes course.

One of the excellent qualities of the parachute spinnaker is that it can be jibed without too much difficulty. The old-fashioned, flat spinnaker usually could not be jibed. It had to be lowered and reset on the other tack. The modern parachute, however, is reversible and the fittings on each end of the pole can be the same so that they can be switched. Figure 53 shows the end-for-end method of the jibing of a 'chute in three steps. The mainsail, left off for simplicity, would be jibed as it normally would, were there no spinnaker.

In step A we see that the guy is slacked slightly and also the lift if the pole is too high to reach, and the inboard end of the pole is unhooked from the mast. This unattached end of the pole is then hooked onto

FIGURE 50: A TURTLE (for medium-size boat)

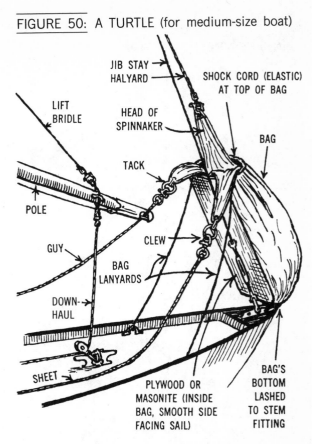

SPINNAKER READY TO HOIST (POLE TO PORT)
Be careful that leeches are not twisted around each other when sail is put into bag. Spinnaker may be hoisted while jib is set, but after spinnaker is up, jib should be lowered.

FIGURE 51:

A STOPPED SPINNAKER (pull on sheet to break it out.)

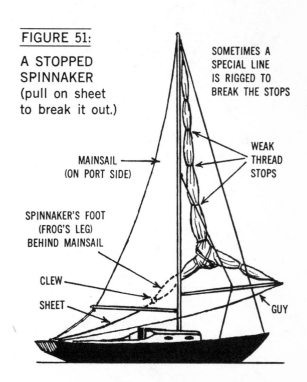

51

SPINNAKER HELMSMANSHIP

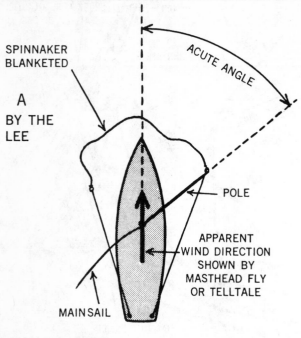

SPINNAKER
BLANKETED

A
BY THE
LEE

ACUTE ANGLE

POLE

APPARENT
WIND DIRECTION
SHOWN BY
MASTHEAD FLY
OR TELLTALE

MAINSAIL

HEAD UP (turn to starboard)

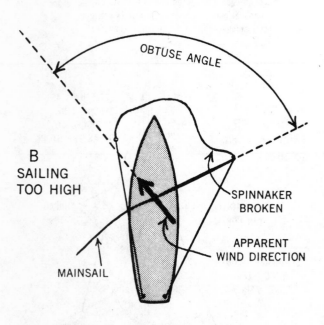

OBTUSE ANGLE

B
SAILING
TOO HIGH

SPINNAKER
BROKEN

APPARENT
WIND DIRECTION

MAINSAIL

BEAR OFF (turn to port)

Masthead flies often swing from side to side
if boat is rolling severely. In such a case it
is usually better to watch the telltales.

the sheet near the clew so that both ends of the pole are fastened near the bottom corners of the spinnaker. At this moment the boat is dead before the wind, the mainsail is being jibed, and the spinnaker remains full and is at right angles to the wind. This is shown in step B. The final step, C, shows the completed jibe. The pole fitting which was originally the only one attached to the sail has now been removed from the spinnaker and is attached to the mast. All lines are left attached as they were (unless the downhaul is rigged from the pole's end instead of its middle). Thus what was formerly the tack with a guy now becomes a clew with its sheet, and what was the clew now becomes the tack. Notice in step C that the guy can be hooked down to avoid the need for the downhaul. Quite often the guy is hauled down with a *twing*, a block at the end of a short line through which the guy or sheet is run. When jibing on a large boat, especially in a fresh breeze, the pole is left attached to the mast and the outboard pole end is released from the tack, dipped down under the headstay, and attached to the spinnaker's clew on the other side of the boat. This method is generally called *dip-pole jibing*.

To take the spinnaker off, we guy the pole all the way forward, release the tack from the guy, and let it fly. When this occurs the boat should be held directly before the wind if possible, so that the spinnaker will be blanketed by the mainsail. This will make the procedure much easier, especially in a strong breeze. Then the sail is slowly lowered by its halyard and pulled in by its sheet into the arms of a crew member, who must "eat it" or bundle it in and sit on the sail or stuff it down a hatch to prevent it from blowing overboard. Here is a tip on lowering the spinnaker: before releasing the tack, be sure the sheet is cleated or knotted so that it won't run through its lead block. If the sheet gets away from you, the entire spinnaker can stream out from the masthead like a flag. This has happened, and your author knows it from firsthand experience!

I don't believe that, as of now, anyone can claim to know everything about the aerodynamics of spinnakers. There is much experimenting with new shapes going on today. The latest thinking is that the best all-around spinnaker is one which is wide in girth but not extremely deep at its center (see Figure 54, A). If the sail's belly is fairly flat, it may be carried closer to the wind when reaching, and it will not trap dead air at its center. On a deep-bellied spinnaker, efficiency-robbing dead air may be trapped even on a reach when the airflow moves across the sail from luff to leech. (See Figure 54, B). Currently in vogue are *tri-radial spinnakers*, those with radial seams at all three corners to minimize excessive stretch when reaching.

FIGURE 53: JIBING THE SPINNAKER (the end-for-end method)

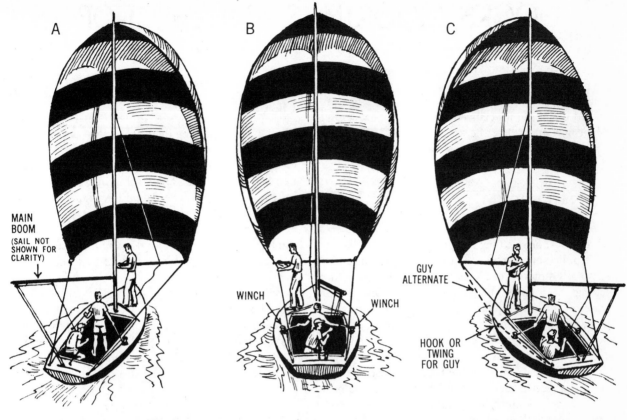

A

MAIN BOOM (SAIL NOT SHOWN FOR CLARITY)

B

WINCH   WINCH

C

GUY ALTERNATE

HOOK OR TWING FOR GUY

LIFT AND GUY SLACKED SLIGHTLY. FORE DECK MAN UNHOOKS POLE FROM MAST. On small boats one man can handle sheet & guy. Each line should be led to and snubbed on (wrapped around) a winch.

SHEET SLACKED SLIGHTLY. POLE END SNAPPED ON SHEET. POLE NOW ON BOTH CORNERS OF SAIL AND AT RIGHT ANGLES TO WIND. HELMSMAN HOLDS BOAT BEFORE WIND AND JIBES THE MAIN. On some small boats fore deck man can work in fore end of cockpit.

POLE UNHOOKED FROM FORMER GUY. NEW GUY (PORT SIDE) IS SLACKED. POLE END HOOKED TO MAST. NEW SHEET TRIMMED IN. On small boats, guy can be hooked down forward near shrouds (shown by dotted line) to hold pole down eliminating need for downhaul.

FIGURE 54: SPINNAKER DRAFT

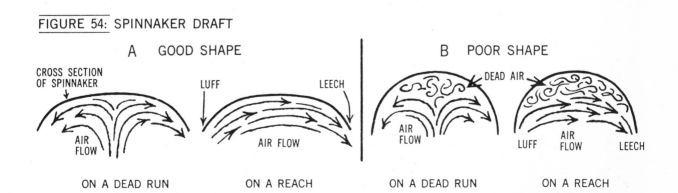

A   GOOD SHAPE

CROSS SECTION OF SPINNAKER

AIR FLOW

ON A DEAD RUN

LUFF   LEECH

AIR FLOW

ON A REACH

B   POOR SHAPE

DEAD AIR

AIR FLOW

ON A DEAD RUN

LUFF   AIR FLOW   LEECH

ON A REACH

DOCKS, MOORINGS, AND ANCHORS

In the previous two sections we have seen how a boat is handled under sail in relatively open water. Now let us look at how and where she is secured and how she is handled in the narrow, crowded waters of an anchorage.

DRY-SAILERS

When not in use, boats are either left afloat at a *mooring** or dock, or else they are pulled out of the water. Those pulled out are often called *dry-sailers*, and they are usually small racers. There are several reasons for keeping these boats out of water. First, there is no danger of their swamping or capsizing in a storm and second, they do not need an antifouling paint, or marine-growth-killing paint, on their bottoms. Antifouling paint is generally not as smooth as the non-antifouling, enamel paints developed for the bottoms of racing dry-sailers. If a racer is made of wood, there is still another good reason for keeping her out of water between races. A wood boat will absorb water, and this will increase her hull weight, causing her to be less competitive.

Dinghies and very small dry-sailers may be pulled out on ramps, floats, or even rough beaches when soft rollers are used to protect the smooth bottoms of the craft. Obviously it is better to keep these boats under a roof if possible, but this is a luxury many boat clubs cannot afford. The next best thing to a roof is a canvas cover to keep off the sun and rain. Larger dry-sailers must be pulled out of the water by hoists or cranes and kept on trailers or *cradles*, wooden structures for the support of boats. There are advantages in having a trailer, for the boat may be towed behind a car to cruise in distant waters or to participate in distant regattas that could not be reached otherwise.

It is my feeling that boats larger than small, open-cockpit racers should be left afloat because a large heavy boat is too troublesome to put in and pull out of the water. Boats that can be launched only with great difficulty will not often be sailed.

Mooring—Technically this term deals with the securing of a vessel with anchors or lines in such a way as to reduce her swinging to wind or tide. However, the term is more commonly used, in yachting circles, when referring to a boat's securing to a permanent-type anchor.

DOCKS

Many sailors who keep their boats afloat prefer to keep them at *docks** for the sake of convenience. However, great care must be taken to see that the boat is properly tied and protected by fenders. Figure 55 shows how a boat is usually tied. The dotted lines represent breast lines which are rarely used except on very large boats or in storms. Whenever possible lines should be led through *chocks*, fairleads for docking lines (see blowup in Figure 55). This is done to reduce chafe, both to the line and to the boat's rail.

Before leaving his boat tied to a dock, a skipper should know about the tide in his area—the range between low and high water for that time of the year. It is important to leave enough slack in his docking lines to allow for his boat rising on a high tide or dropping on a low tide.

Dock—The space between piers in which vessels are berthed or the pier itself.

FIGURE 55: DOCK LINES

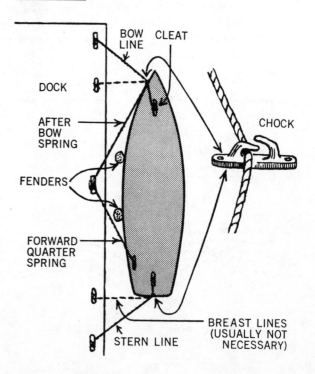

FIGURE 56: FENDERBOARD

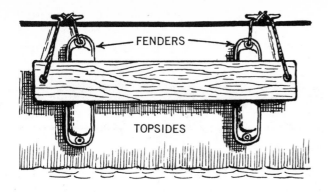

FENDERS

TOPSIDES

FIGURE 57: APPROACHING A DOCK UNDER SAIL (in weak current)

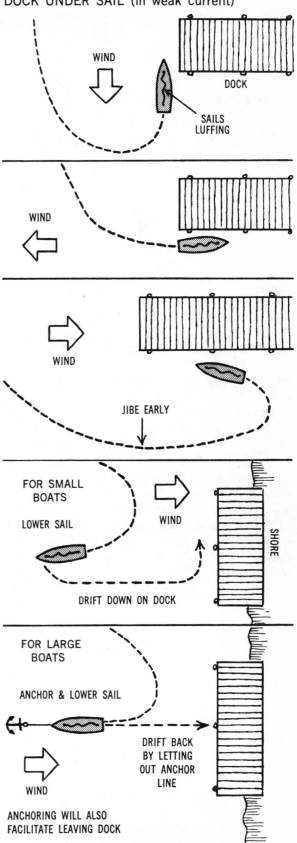

WIND

DOCK

SAILS LUFFING

WIND

WIND

JIBE EARLY

FOR SMALL BOATS

LOWER SAIL

WIND

SHORE

DRIFT DOWN ON DOCK

FOR LARGE BOATS

ANCHOR & LOWER SAIL

WIND

DRIFT BACK BY LETTING OUT ANCHOR LINE

ANCHORING WILL ALSO FACILITATE LEAVING DOCK

Rigging fenders or bumpers often presents a problem at a dock having *piles* (wharf posts) which extend beyond the edge of the dock, because a fender will often roll off the pile against which it has been resting and allow the topsides to get scarred. A simple solution to this problem is a *sideboard* or *fenderboard*, as shown in Figure 56.

Landing at a dock under sail requires caution and planning. Here is an important rule: Unless there is a strong current against the wind, approach a dock from the leeward side whenever possible so that your boat is headed into the wind (see Figure 57). The diagram shows that the boat is turned into the wind and also that as the dock is approached, there is nothing dead ahead of the boat's bow. The purpose of turning into the wind is to make the boat's sails flap in order to kill her speed. The only exception to this would be if a strong current were running against the wind. In this case, which would probably not happen very often, the dock should be approached on a run from the wind-ward side under shortened sail, usually with jib alone, to reduce speed. Immediately prior to landing, the sail would be lowered to kill headway. If, for some reason, you have to approach a wharf from its windward side, you must lower sail before landing as shown in the diagrams.

When a boat is turned into the wind so that she may coast up to a dock or mooring, the maneuver is called *shooting*. If the turn is made slowly, the boat will *carry a lot of way* or coast a long distance, but if the helm is jammed over hard, this will kill the boat's way and cause her to stop in a short distance. Just how much way a boat carries depends primarily on her size and weight. A skipper must get to know his own boat.

Occasionally it is necessary, due to crowded condi-tions, to land in the middle of a dock so that the bow is aimed directly at the dock. This type of approach could be quite dangerous for a beginner in a large, heavy boat, and I would not advise his trying it unless abso-lutely necessary. In a small light boat, however, this

FIGURE 58: LEAVING A DOCK

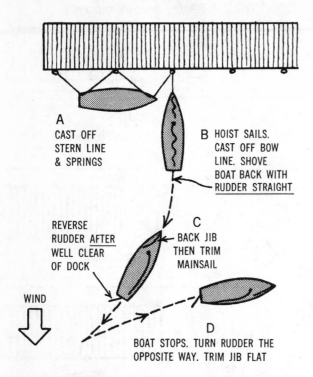

A
CAST OFF
STERN LINE
& SPRINGS

B HOIST SAILS.
CAST OFF BOW
LINE. SHOVE
BOAT BACK WITH
RUDDER STRAIGHT

REVERSE
RUDDER AFTER
WELL CLEAR
OF DOCK

C
BACK JIB
THEN TRIM
MAINSAIL

WIND

D
BOAT STOPS. TURN RUDDER THE
OPPOSITE WAY. TRIM JIB FLAT

kind of landing is quite common, but it is done with caution. The dock should be approached at a moderate speed with sails slightly luffing, and the shoot should be made from sufficient distance away from the dock so that if it is found that the boat has too much way, she can be borne off before striking the dock. Ideally the boat should stop dead just as she reaches the dock, but this requires perfect timing, and there are many variables that could throw off this timing, such as a strong wind or current. A crew member should be stationed in the bow with a neatly coiled bow line. If the boat has slightly too much way, the crewman can sit on the bow with his legs straddling the jib stay where he can fend off with his feet. His legs should be far enough apart, on either side of the pointed bow, so that his feet can't get crushed between the boat and wharf.

When getting ready to leave a dock, try to have your boat heading into the wind. About the only time when this might not be possible would be if the boat were controlled by a strong current. Any other time, sails should be hoisted with the boat head to wind. If you are on the lee side of the dock, lying beam to the breeze with no excessive current, slack off your stern and spring lines so that the boat swings around into the wind (see boat in Figure 58). If you happen to be on the dock's windward side, you must, before hoisting sail, get away from the dock. This might be accomplished by paddling, motoring, *warping* (moving the boat with lines), or *kedging* (moving by putting out an anchor and pulling up to it). But the important thing is

to get your bow at least close to the wind before hoisting sail.

When you are ready to get under way or cast off your bow line, have a crew member on the bow push the boat backwards, away from the dock and in the direction you wish to turn. Remember from your experience in getting out of stays that when the boat is moving backwards the helm must be reversed, turned the opposite way it would be turned were the boat moving forward (see Figure 58). As soon as the boat stops drifting backwards and gains headway, handle the helm as it normally would be handled.

One word of caution: When leaving or approaching a dock, watch your boom. If it is off, be careful not to let its sheet get hooked over a pile or get fouled on another boat.

MOORINGS AND ANCHORS

In spite of the fact that leaving a boat on a mooring is often less convenient than lying alongside a dock, I prefer the mooring which anchors the boat out in a harbor. There it is more private, easier to get under way, usually cooler with fewer insects, and there is less chance of marring the topsides. A boat left swinging to a mooring can nearly always be better ventilated, because if the harbor is a good one without strong currents, the boat will lie head to the wind. This means that on most cabin boats, the after, vertical opening of the companionway hatch may be closed with an open louvered slide, because rain, blown by the wind, will slant aft, away from the hatch opening. Likewise, open boats without self-bailing cockpits may be fitted with cockpit covers that are open at the after end.

Figure 59 shows a permanent mooring which is comprised of a small pickup float, a pendant, a buoy, a light chain, a heavy chain, and a permanent-type anchor. Pickup floats are varied in design, but they should be soft enough not to scratch a boat and have firm loops so that the float can be picked up easily with a *boat hook*, which is simply a pole with a hook at one end (see Figure 59). Many floats are of light wood, plastic, or cork with rope loops on top. Mooring buoys also come in a variety of styles. The one illustrated has padding around its middle so it will not scratch a boat's hull. Some modern pickup floats are fitted with staffs or short plastic masts sticking up above the water so that the float can be picked up without a boat hook.

When a mooring float is picked up, it is pulled aboard the boat, the pendant is pulled up, and its loop is put over the heavy bow cleat. Incidentally, bow cleats and *bitts* (heavy posts used for making fast tow lines or mooring cables) should be securely bolted to structural members. The lower end of the light chain is attached to the heavy chain by a heavy swivel (see the blowup in

FIGURE 59: A MOORING

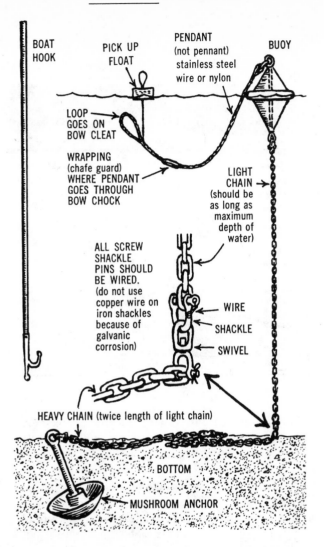

BOAT HOOK

PICK UP FLOAT

PENDANT (not pennant) stainless steel wire or nylon

BUOY

LOOP GOES ON BOW CLEAT

WRAPPING (chafe guard) WHERE PENDANT GOES THROUGH BOW CHOCK

LIGHT CHAIN (should be as long as maximum depth of water)

ALL SCREW SHACKLE PINS SHOULD BE WIRED. (do not use copper wire on iron shackles because of galvanic corrosion)

WIRE

SHACKLE

SWIVEL

HEAVY CHAIN (twice length of light chain)

BOTTOM

MUSHROOM ANCHOR

Figure 59). If screw shackles are used with this arrangement, their screw pins should be wired in place because in time, they can unscrew themselves. This has happened many times! The purpose of the heavy chain is not only to provide strength, but also to give added weight and to act as a shock absorber when the moored boat is *pitching*, or rocking from bow to stern, in a heavy sea.

The anchor itself is usually a *mushroom anchor*, so called because it looks like an upside-down mushroom. This type of anchor sinks deep down into the sand or mud, not immediately and sometimes not until several weeks after it strikes bottom. Once entirely buried, however, it has tremendous holding power. By keeping his anchor line secured to a buoy, a skipper may take his boat to and from a heavy permanent-type anchor without having to pull his anchor up every time he takes his boat out.

Figure 60 shows several types of nonpermanent an-

chors with their various parts named. These anchors are carried on board and used when a boat is to be anchored temporarily. A day sailer should always carry at least one anchor, and it is a wise practice for every cabin cruiser to carry at least two, one light and one heavy. Most anchors are designed so that when they are pulled along the bottom at a certain angle, their flukes will dig into the bottom. The stock keeps an anchor from turning over on its side in a position where the flukes cannot dig in.

FIGURE 60: ANCHORS

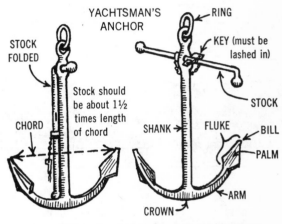

YACHTSMAN'S ANCHOR

STOCK FOLDED

CHORD

RING

KEY (must be lashed in)

STOCK

SHANK

FLUKE

BILL

PALM

ARM

CROWN

Stock should be about 1½ times length of chord

Wide palms for mud or soft sand bottoms. Sharp, narrow palms for hard sand, rock, weed, gravel, or shell.

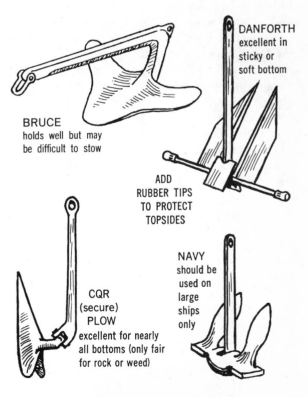

BRUCE holds well but may be difficult to stow

DANFORTH excellent in sticky or soft bottom

ADD RUBBER TIPS TO PROTECT TOPSIDES

CQR (secure) PLOW excellent for nearly all bottoms (only fair for rock or weed)

NAVY should be used on large ships only

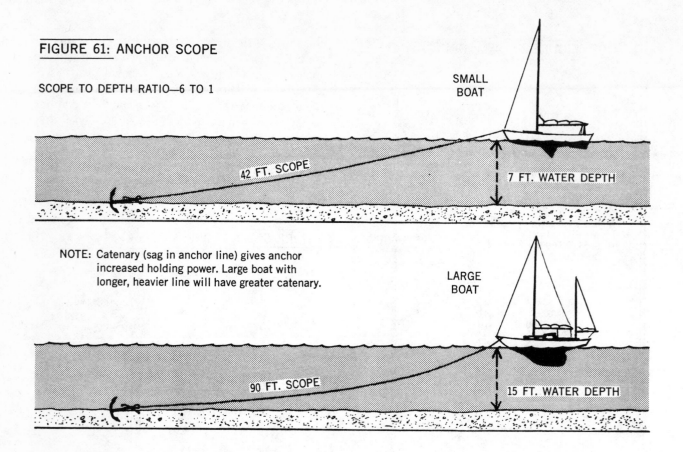

FIGURE 61: ANCHOR SCOPE

SCOPE TO DEPTH RATIO—6 TO 1

SMALL BOAT

42 FT. SCOPE

7 FT. WATER DEPTH

NOTE: Catenary (sag in anchor line) gives anchor increased holding power. Large boat with longer, heavier line will have greater catenary.

LARGE BOAT

90 FT. SCOPE

15 FT. WATER DEPTH

The chief factors that determine the holding power of an anchor are its weight and the *scope* or length of its anchor line. The greater the weight and the longer the scope, the greater the holding power. The ideal length of scope is generally said to be six or seven times the depth of water where the boat is anchored. However, this ideal is usually difficult to achieve because of the crowded conditions of most anchorages today. A boat must have sufficient *swinging room*, which means that she must be far enough away from the other boats at anchor to clear them no matter what the direction of the wind and current. The greater a boat's scope, the greater her circle of swing will be. In a crowded harbor, to save space, small boats should anchor close to shore in fairly shallow water. This will also save scope for the small craft, because the important factor is the ratio of water depth to length of scope. If one is shortened, then the other may be shortened without changing the ratio. This is demonstrated in Figure 61. The small boat with short scope has the same ratio, six to one, as the large boat. However, the large boat, with more scope and heavier line, has the greater catenary or sag in her line, and this somewhat increases her anchor's holding power.

There are some general rules for the weight and size of *ground tackle**, but they are not suitable for the

beginning sailor because they have many variables and exceptions depending on the kind of anchor, type of bottom, and so forth. There is, however, a very simple, easy-to-remember rule of thumb that the novice may keep in mind as a rough guide for weight of anchors. This is simply that with permanent-type anchors, there should be about ten pounds of anchor for every foot of overall length. (For example, a boat 35 feet overall would take a 350-pound mooring.) For a regular, non-permanent anchor, the rule of thumb is one pound for each foot of overall length, while for a "lunch hook," light anchor, it is a half-pound per foot. Some sailors might think that the rule for permanent anchors is unnecessarily great with a mushroom in a protected harbor, but mooring lines seem to be getting shorter and shorter in many harbors around the country due to crowded conditions; hence when the scope is decreased, the weight of anchor must be increased.

Actually, the size and kind of anchor as well as how much anchor line you carry will depend on a number of factors, including (1) the weight of your boat as well as her length; (2) her *windage* or resistance to the wind caused by freeboard, cabin house, and rigging; (3) the amount of tide and current in your area; (4) the amount of protection the harbors in your area afford; (5) the average depth of water in those harbors or wherever you might be forced to anchor; and (6) the kinds of bottoms in those harbors. The best holding

---

*Ground tackle—general term for anchors and related gear.

bottom is generally sticky mud or a combination of mud and clay. Sand, gravel, or grass-covered bottoms are fairly good for holding the anchor once it is thoroughly dug in, but soft mud is poor for holding. An anchor will often skid along a rocky bottom until its fluke or flukes become lodged in a crevice. Then it may hold very well but be difficult to break out. When anchoring in rocky waters, it is often wise to rig a tripping line tied to the anchor's crown so it can be lifted up by its bottom end if a fluke gets stuck (see Figure 62).

Of the various kinds of anchors, the traditional yachtsman's type is still popular, but it has one drawback. When one fluke is buried, the other sticks up and is apt to get fouled by the anchor line. This can happen if the boat is carried by wind or current so that she makes a circle or swings one-and-a-half times around

her anchor (see Figure 63). When this happens the anchor has no holding power.

In selecting an anchorage, try to pick one without excessive currents, because if the breeze becomes light, the boat's heading will be dominated by the current and this will cause her to swing around a great deal on her anchor line as she is alternately controlled by wind and current. In this case her anchor line is highly susceptible to fouling.

Always carry more than enough anchor line, because scope is tremendously important to an anchor's holding power. For convenience, it is good to carry a short, light line for temporary anchoring in fair weather, but you should also have a heavy, extra-long line for heavy weather. As for the anchor line material, most sailors prefer nylon because it resists rot and has a lot of stretch, which reduces shock loading in rough water,

FIGURE 62: TRIP LINE

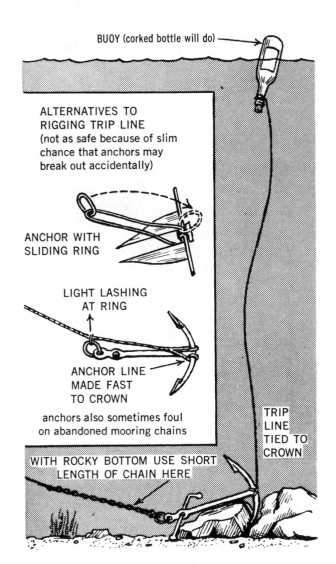

BUOY (corked bottle will do)

ALTERNATIVES TO RIGGING TRIP LINE
(not as safe because of slim chance that anchors may break out accidentally)

ANCHOR WITH SLIDING RING

LIGHT LASHING AT RING

ANCHOR LINE MADE FAST TO CROWN

anchors also sometimes foul on abandoned mooring chains

WITH ROCKY BOTTOM USE SHORT LENGTH OF CHAIN HERE

TRIP LINE TIED TO CROWN

FIGURE 63: FOULED ANCHOR

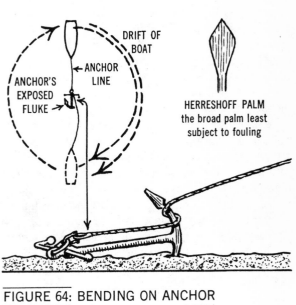

DRIFT OF BOAT

ANCHOR'S EXPOSED FLUKE

ANCHOR LINE

HERRESHOFF PALM
the broad palm least subject to fouling

FIGURE 64: BENDING ON ANCHOR LINE

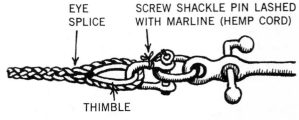

EYE SPLICE

SCREW SHACKLE PIN LASHED WITH MARLINE (HEMP CORD)

THIMBLE

ON MOORING LINES THIMBLE SHOULD BE WIRED IN PLACE.
(don't use copper wire on galvanized thimble)

which can break the anchor loose. A short length of chain between the anchor and *rode* (anchor line) will increase the anchor's weight and catenary and also help prevent chafe on a rocky or coral-covered bottom.

The anchor line may be made fast to the anchor ring by a fisherman's bend (see Figure 69), but it is better to use an eye splice with a metal thimble and a shackle as illustrated in Figure 64. This will reduce chafe. The pin in the shackle should be tied with heavy string so that it will not back out or unscrew itself.

When coming to anchor under sail without excessive current, the proper procedure is to hold your boat into the wind with sails shaking until all forward motion has stopped. Then after the anchor is made ready and secured to its line, it is carefully lowered from the bow. When the anchor's crown touches bottom, the boat should be drifting backwards. If you have an auxiliary, run your engine in reverse. Then the line is *paid out* slowly. Care should be taken not to pay out the line too rapidly, because this can cause it to foul the anchor. Keep a slight tension on the line as the boat drifts backwards. Scope is let out until the anchor can bite into the bottom. Then the line is *snubbed*, or stopped from running out, by a turn on the bow cleat. This should cause the anchor to dig into the bottom and, of course, stop the boat from drifting back. When you are sure the anchor is properly dug in, let out all the scope you can, which will still leave you plenty of swinging room.

To break out the anchor, you must pull in on the line until it lies straight up and down so that the boat is directly over the anchor. Then a hard pull on the line will lift up the anchor's head in much the same manner that a pick ax is broken out of the ground by lifting straight up on its handle. If your boat has an auxiliary, the anchor can usually be broken out with ease after the line is straight up and down by merely driving the boat, under engine, directly ahead. If the anchor is very difficult to break out, here is a neat trick which often works on small boats: The crew moves forward while the line is pulled in as far as possible and cleated. Then the crew moves aft. This shifting of weight aft makes the bow lift up and break out the anchor.

Getting under way from a mooring or anchor involves many of the same basic principles as leaving a dock. It is nearly always best to have your boat heading into the wind when hoisting sail. This is usually true even if you are under auxiliary power. A mainsail hoisted with the wind from astern, for instance, is blown against the shrouds, and it is very apt to foul and be ripped as it is pulled up.

There is at least one time, however, when it is advisable to hoist a sail downwind. This is when an anchored boat's heading is controlled by a strong current

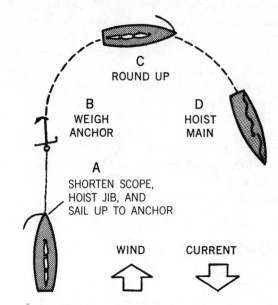

FIGURE 65: GETTING UNDER WAY

(strong current against the wind)

C ROUND UP

B WEIGH ANCHOR

D HOIST MAIN

A SHORTEN SCOPE, HOIST JIB, AND SAIL UP TO ANCHOR

WIND

CURRENT

BOAT AT ANCHOR LYING TO CURRENT INSTEAD OF WIND

flowing against the wind. Such a situation would probably be rare in most of our country's best harbors; nevertheless, here is the recommended method of getting under way when this condition of wind and current exists (see Figure 65): First the jib is slowly hoisted to move the boat over her anchor, which is *weighed* or pulled up. Then the jib sheet is slacked and the boat rounded up into the wind as far as possible, after which the main is hoisted. If the boat is moored, she must run under her jib a considerable distance beyond her cast-off mooring float before rounding up to hoist her main so that she won't be set back on the float by the current.

If a boat is coming to anchor or picking up her mooring under these conditions, the same procedure is followed, but in reverse. The main is lowered while the boat is heading into the wind to windward of the mooring float or desired anchoring location. Then the boat is run before the wind under her jib alone against the current until she reaches the float or anchoring spot, at which time the jib is immediately lowered and the float is picked up or the anchor lowered.

Normally, however, when the current is either weak or with the wind, a boat is luffed into the wind and shot for her mooring as she would be when landing at a dock. When getting under way in normal conditions with the boat's bow to wind, the aftermost sails are hoisted first to keep the bow from being blown off. On a yawl or ketch, the mizzen is often sheeted in flat to hold the boat into the wind while the other sails are being hoisted. Before casting off the mooring or weighing anchor in a crowded anchorage, plan your course carefully. Figure which tack will give the most room for maneuvering. Remember that you must have ample room to bear off to gain headway. You may make the boat bear off on the proper tack by backing the jib, the way you would if you were in stays (described in Section VII). The jib is held to windward on the side opposite from that toward which you wish the bow to swing. In other words, if you want to be on the starboard tack, the jib is backed to starboard and vice versa (see Figure 34, A).

Here are some general tips for maneuvering in crowded harbors:

(1) Keep plenty of way on at all times. Without way a boat can easily get in stays, and this can be more than embarrassing in a well-populated harbor. A boat must be moving to be maneuverable.

(2) Practice shooting your boat to see how far she will carry, but do this first in open waters away from other boats.

(3) Allow for at least some stern skid. A boat does not turn like an automobile with the rear following the front. A boat's bow turns in one direction while her stern skids the opposite way. Of course this varies with individual boats. A shallow-bottomed centerboarder with short rudder and little *skeg** usually skids the most. But, once again, get to know your own boat.

(4) Enter the harbor with a fairly shortened but well-balanced sail plan. Don't carry large Genoa jibs or the like which would give you too much speed and not enough maneuverability. If your boat will balance fairly well without her jib, take it down. However, if your boat is a cutter with a large head rig she may have too much weather helm with no jib; so set a small working staysail for balance before going into the anchorage.

(5) Don't cut too close to other boats or drop your sails before picking up the mooring. When passing near other boats, remember that they have anchor cables extending out under the water. One occasionally sees experienced sailors shoot for a mooring and drop all sails before picking up the float, but this is not for the beginner, and it can be risky for anyone.

(6) If you find that you have too much way on after picking up the mooring, try backing the main. Push the main boom all the way forward so that the sail will be aback and the boat will stop and, with the rudder turned the proper way, will begin to move backwards. Workboat skippers often use this trick effectively.

---

*Skeg—An after, downward extension of the keel which usually supports the bottom of the rudder.

LEAVING YOUR BOAT

After your mooring has been picked up, sails should be lowered from forward to aft so that a forward sail will not fill and blow the bow off, causing your boat to swing around excessively on her mooring. Everyone in the cockpit should watch out for the main boom swinging back and forth. Before lowering the mainsail, be sure the topping lift is set up tight so that the boom will not drop down on the deck when the sail is lowered. As previously mentioned, sails should be unbent and stowed in bags if possible. Otherwise they should be furled, well-stopped, and then protected with sail covers (described in Section V).

Before leaving your boat, have her shipshape. People will get a poor impression of your seamanship if they see lines uncoiled, slatting around, and hanging over the side; if they see your boom not secured but swinging to and fro; or your tiller swinging back and forth banging the cockpit coaming. These things are obviously not good for your boat.

Here is a rough checklist of what should be done every time you leave your boat for any length of time:

(1) See that the mooring line is properly secured. If your boat is alongside a dock, see that she is properly made fast and fendered. All lines should be led through chocks, and if there is a possibility of chafe, the lines should be protected with wrappings of canvas or a rubber-hose type of chafe preventer (see Figure 66). With a mooring line, it is wise to lash the line's loop onto the bow cleat or bitt to be sure that the loop won't jump off in a storm. This can often be done by simply cleating the line that secures the pickup float over the top of the pendant's loop.

(2) Unbend sails or furl and cover. This has been discussed.

(3) Pump bilge and remove scupper plugs. Some

FIGURE 66: CHAFE GUARDS

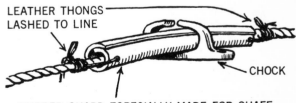

LEATHER THONGS LASHED TO LINE

CHOCK

RUBBER GUARD ESPECIALLY MADE FOR CHAFE

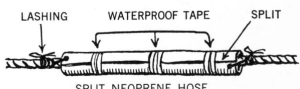

LASHING   WATERPROOF TAPE   SPLIT

SPLIT NEOPRENE HOSE

FIGURE 67: VENTILATION AT MOORINGS

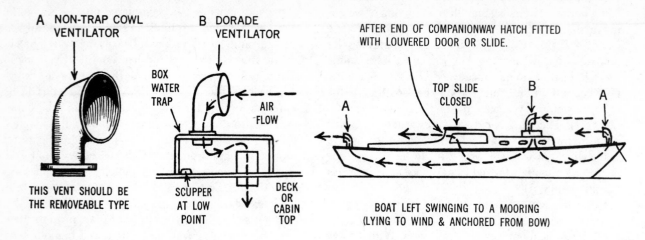

A NON-TRAP COWL
    VENTILATOR

THIS VENT SHOULD BE
THE REMOVEABLE TYPE

B DORADE
    VENTILATOR

BOX
WATER
TRAP

AIR
FLOW

SCUPPER
AT LOW
POINT

DECK
OR
CABIN
TOP

AFTER END OF COMPANIONWAY HATCH FITTED
WITH LOUVERED DOOR OR SLIDE.

TOP SLIDE
CLOSED

BOAT LEFT SWINGING TO A MOORING
(LYING TO WIND & ANCHORED FROM BOW)

boats with self-bailing cockpits have scupper plugs to prevent water from coming in when the boat is heeled over a great deal. These must be removed when at anchor or else rainwater will not run out.

(4) See that your boat is covered or closed, but ventilated. Small open boats should have cockpit covers to keep out rainwater. Large cabin boats should have all hatches not only closed but fastened closed, because a small twister can lift off a hatch cover. Regular cowl-type ventilators should be turned aft to keep out rainwater, but the trap type often called *Dorade vents** should face forward for maximum air (see Figure 67) when a boat is lying at a mooring.

(5) All lines should be coiled. (This will be dealt with in the next section.) Pull taut all halyards and sheets—then cleat them securely. Halyards should be tied away from the mast to keep them from slapping the mast in a breeze. This can chafe the mast and the sound will be annoying to people on nearby boats.

(6) Unship your rudder or take it off and stow it in

the cockpit if you have a small boat with an outboard rudder. On a large boat lash the tiller to keep it from swinging around. Most experienced sailors agree that the centerboard should be left all the way up for several reasons. First, if the board is up, it will not work back and forth and bump against the side of its well. This could loosen the well and possibly cause a leak. Second, the board, when kept up, will not attract barnacles, worms, and marine growth. If a boat is so flat-bottomed that she ranges around on her mooring or yaws back and forth excessively, then her board might be lowered slightly to give her a little lateral resistance, which would retard this motion.

(7) Stow all loose gear below, under the fore deck or in the stern locker. Lash anything that is too sizeable to stow. Cut off the battery at the main switch if you have electricity, and cut off the gas valve from your fuel tank if you have an auxiliary. Check the intake valve on the head to be sure it is cut off. A leaking head could sink the boat in your absence.

Dorade vents—Carried by *Dorade*, one of the first of the modern-type ocean racers.

SECTION X

BASIC MARLINSPIKE SEAMANSHIP

ROPE

At this point, the reader must be growing aware of the importance of rope. It is used for controlling the sails, docking, mooring, anchoring, and for just about everything done on a boat. The beginner should have at least a basic knowledge of how to use and care for rope. This includes knowing the most commonly used knots as well as at least one kind of splice and how to *whip* a line, or finish off its end with thread to prevent unraveling.

Rope is a general term for wires or fibers twisted or woven together. (Of course, as previously mentioned, ropes are generally called lines when used on a boat.) For yachts at least, the most commonly used fiber ropes are those made of synthetics, especially Dacron, nylon, and Kevlar sheathed with Dacron. These materials have many advantages over sisal, manila, and other vegetable fibers in strength, durability, and resistance to swelling. Also, Dacron and Kevlar are much more resistant to stretch. The drawback with Kevlar is that it can fatigue quite easily when sharply bent repeatedly while under strain, and so it must be bent over special sheaves of extra-large diameter. Nylon is relatively elastic. This characteristic makes it good for anchor lines, *painters* (permanent bow lines on small boats), dock lines, and tow lines, but elasticity is very undesirable for sheets and halyards.

Rope, if not braided, is made by twisting the fibers into yarns, which are combined and twisted into strands. These are again combined and twisted the opposite way into rope. Fibers are usually twisted to the right to form yarns, yarns to the left to form strands, strands to the right to form ropes. Such ropes are said to be *laid* right-handed, meaning that their strands are twisted to the right. To avoid kinks, a right-laid line should be coiled clockwise, from left to right (see Figure 68). A light line may be held with one hand and coiled with the other, but a heavy line must be placed on the deck and coiled by winding it around in great loops, one on top of the other. The diagram also shows how to hang a coiled halyard on its cleat. For best sailing efficiency, many racing skippers keep these coils lower to the deck than shown in the diagram. High coils may make windage or cause eddies in the air flow near the mainsail's foot. The purpose of coiling a line is not only for appearance but also for convenience and safety. An uncoiled line can easily become knotted, kinked, or fouled.

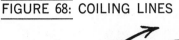

FIGURE 68: COILING LINES

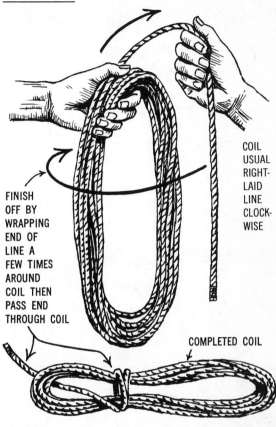

COIL USUAL RIGHT-LAID LINE CLOCKWISE

FINISH OFF BY WRAPPING END OF LINE A FEW TIMES AROUND COIL THEN PASS END THROUGH COIL

COMPLETED COIL

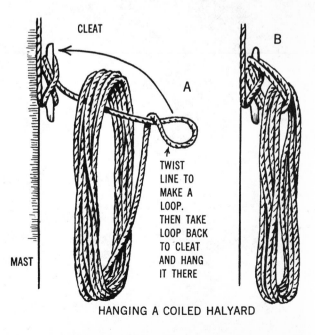

CLEAT

B

A

MAST

TWIST LINE TO MAKE A LOOP. THEN TAKE LOOP BACK TO CLEAT AND HANG IT THERE

HANGING A COILED HALYARD

Vegetable-fiber rope should be thoroughly dry before stowage, for dampness can cause it to rot. With the synthetics, this is not necessary for the life of the rope; however, repeated stowage of wet rope in closed lockers on wood boats can cause rot to the wood after a period of time. All lines should be checked periodically for deterioration. Look for cuts and evidence of chafe. Untwist the lines to look inside between the strands. Colorless, powdery, or broken fibers inside mean trouble; so play it safe and get a replacement.

KNOTS, BENDS, AND HITCHES

Figure 69 shows a group of knots, bends, and hitches used for tying a line to itself, another line, or some object. The four most useful are the *square knot*, the *bowline*, *two half hitches*, and the *clove hitch*. A good sailor should know how to tie these blindfolded. The square knot, often called *reef knot*, serves many purposes: tying stops and sail covers, tying in battens, reefing, lashing or securing objects to the deck, and so forth. It consists merely of an overhand knot (Figure 69) followed by another overhand, but care should be taken to see that it is a true square and not a granny (also shown in the diagram) because the latter can easily slip.

The bowline is rightfully called "the king of knots." Its outstanding feature is that, although it will never slip, it will not jam. If correctly tied, the knot is always easy to untie when not under strain. It is used, in general, to fasten a line to an object or to make a temporary loop in the end of a line. The diagram shows a simple, rapid method of tying a bowline. The line is put around the object to which it is to be tied and a simple overhand knot is made. The end of the line is pulled hard, which converts the overhead knot into a

FIGURE 69: KNOTS, BENDS & HITCHES   (All knots are shown tied loosely for clarity, but they should be pulled tight.)

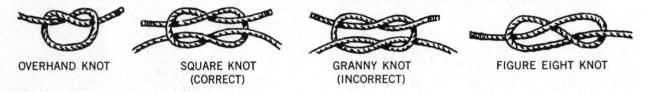

OVERHAND KNOT   SQUARE KNOT (CORRECT)   GRANNY KNOT (INCORRECT)   FIGURE EIGHT KNOT

A QUICK, SURE WAY TO TIE A BOWLINE

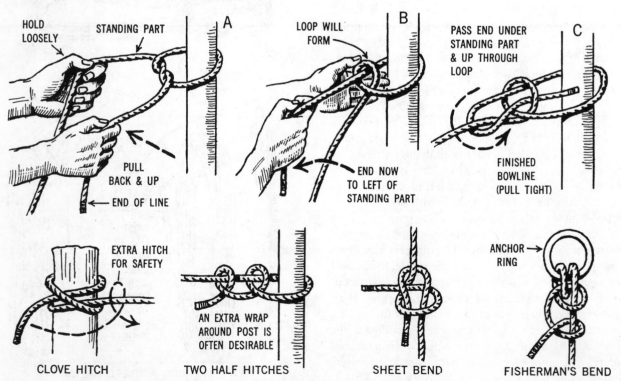

loop through which the end of the line runs. The end is then passed under its standing part (the part which is not the end), around, and back through the loop. As one says when teaching the knot to children, "The rabbit comes out of the hole, runs around the tree, and goes back down the hole." The important thing to remember is that the line's end should go into the loop the same way it came out.

The clove hitch is used chiefly to tie a line to a post or pile. A skillful sailor, when making his dinghy fast to a dock, can throw the loops over the top of a pile as fast as a cowboy can hitch his horse to a rail. For extra security, the line's end should be half-hitched to its standing part as shown in the diagram.

All the remaining knots shown in the diagram are used for specific purposes. The *figure eight* knots the end of a line to prevent it from running through a block; the *fisherman's bend* makes a line fast to the ring of an anchor; and the *sheet bend* fastens the ends of two lines together.

WHIPPING AND SPLICING

Nothing gives a boat a more lubberly appearance than lines unraveling at their ends. These are called *cow's tails* or *Irish pennants*. The solution to this problem is a whipping, which is the wrapping of a line's end with heavy thread. There are several methods of doing this, but the one illustrated in Figure 70, called *needle whipping*, is probably the most permanent. This method requires a heavy sailmaker's needle and twine. For maximum permanency, the twine should be waxed by running it across a cake of bee's wax several times. The needle, after being threaded, is pushed between two strands near the line's end. The thread is then pulled not quite all the way through, its remaining end being flattened against and running in the direction of the line as shown in the diagram. Then the thread is wound around and around the line for a dozen or more times, covering the thread's end, after which the needle is pushed between the strands again. The thread is then pulled back across the wound thread following the lay of the line or the hollows between the strands, and the needle is pushed through the strands again. This process is repeated back and forth across the wound thread along the lay until you end up where you started and finally the thread is knotted and cut. This sounds complicated, but I think the diagram will explain it. The line is then cut off cleanly about one-quarter inch beyond the whipping. After whipping Dacron or nylon, it is a neat trick to fuse the fibers at the line's ragged end with the heat from a match, but this must be done with great care so that the flame will not touch the whipping thread.

There are several different kinds of splices, but the one used most often is the eye splice. This is important when you want a permanent loop in a line or want a line to be bent permanently onto some object like a shackle or spar. Where a rope fastening is to be permanent, a splice will have up to 95 percent of the rope's strength, while many knots can cut a rope's strength by 50 percent.

Splicing a new, heavy line can be hard work, so you should use a *marlinspike* or *fid*. These are short spikes tapered to a point, the former made of metal and the latter of wood. These spikes are forced between the

FIGURE 70: WHIPPING

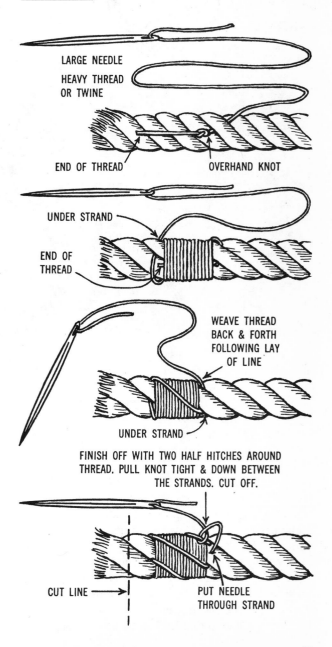

LARGE NEEDLE
HEAVY THREAD
OR TWINE

END OF THREAD   OVERHAND KNOT

UNDER STRAND

END OF THREAD

WEAVE THREAD BACK & FORTH FOLLOWING LAY OF LINE

UNDER STRAND

FINISH OFF WITH TWO HALF HITCHES AROUND THREAD. PULL KNOT TIGHT & DOWN BETWEEN THE STRANDS. CUT OFF.

CUT LINE →   PUT NEEDLE THROUGH STRAND

FIGURE 71: EYE SPLICE (the first series of tucks)

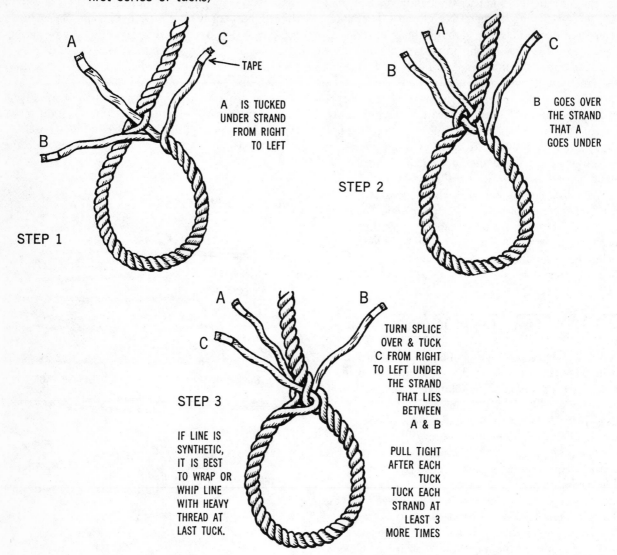

A IS TUCKED UNDER STRAND FROM RIGHT TO LEFT

TAPE

STEP 1

B GOES OVER THE STRAND THAT A GOES UNDER

STEP 2

STEP 3

IF LINE IS SYNTHETIC, IT IS BEST TO WRAP OR WHIP LINE WITH HEAVY THREAD AT LAST TUCK.

TURN SPLICE OVER & TUCK C FROM RIGHT TO LEFT UNDER THE STRAND THAT LIES BETWEEN A & B

PULL TIGHT AFTER EACH TUCK TUCK EACH STRAND AT LEAST 3 MORE TIMES

strands of a line to separate them so that the ends of strands may be pushed through and interwoven.

With an eye splice, the first series of tucks or interweavings of the strands are the most difficult, but I think it will be clear if the diagram in Figure 71 is followed closely. To begin, the three strands are unlaid or unraveled and each of their ends is lightly lashed, whipped, or bound with tape. Then the line is looped so that the strand ends are brought back upon the standing part of the rope. The middle strand ending, designated as A in the diagram, is pushed through two strands which have been opened up on the standing part of the rope. Then strand B, to the left of A, goes over the strand that A goes under, and B goes under the next strand. The next step is the most difficult for beginners. The splice is turned over and C is tucked through the strand that lies between the strands which

A and B are tucked through. The next series of tucks is relatively simple. It is simply a weaving operation in which A, B, and C each go over their next strand and under their following strand. Just make sure that no two strand ends go through the same strand openings, and you cannot go wrong. After three complete series of tucks, the splice can be tapered for a neat appearance. This is done by cutting about half the fibers out of each strand before a final tuck is made. If splicing nylon, put in several extra tucks because of the slipperiness of the material.

Splicing a braided line, which is plaited into rope by machine, normally requires special tools consisting of a tube-like hollow fid and a pusher rod. These tools can be obtained from a *chandlery* (boat store) in kit form with an instruction booklet that adequately explains how to make the splice.

66

WEATHER AND HEAVY-WEATHER SAILING

Every sailor ought to know at least a little about weather, not only to be alert to the approach of storms, but also to be able to predict and take advantage of changes in local conditions of wind and water. He should know something about the general weather pattern, weather maps, the barometer, weather signs in the sky including cloud identification; and most important, he should make a study of local weather behavior.

THE WEATHER MAP AND BAROMETER

The weather map, published daily in most leading newspapers and frequently presented on television, gives a good picture of weather all over the United States. It shows conditions of wind, temperature, and atmospheric pressure. The entire weather pattern in our latitudes tends to move roughly from west to east covering as much as six hundred miles a day but often considerably less, particularly in the summer. If you are planning a cruise, look at the weather map on the day before you leave. Study carefully the weather to the west of you, because that is very likely the weather you will be getting within the next day or so.

Shown on a weather map are the centers of low and high atmospheric pressure. The location of these centers is of the utmost importance in weather prediction. In the northern hemisphere, winds blow around a "high" in a clockwise direction away from its center. This is called an *anti-cyclonic rotation*. Winds blow around a "low," however, in a counterclockwise direction toward its center. This is a *cyclonic rotation*. Fair weather is usually associated with a high, and bad weather with a low. The air flow moves from a high-pressure area into a low (see Figure 72). The curved solid lines which run around and between the high and low centers on a weather map are called *isobars*. These lines connect points of equal atmospheric pressure. Where isobars run close together, the winds are usually high in velocity; but where isobars are far apart, winds are generally mild.

A weather map will also show some lines with small triangular shapes on one side (saw-toothed), other lines with round bumps on one side, and still others with a combination of round bumps and triangles. These lines are symbols for the four kinds of *fronts: cold, warm, stationary,* and *occluded* (see Figure 73). Fronts occur where two air masses of different temperatures collide.

FIGURE 72: HIGHS & LOWS

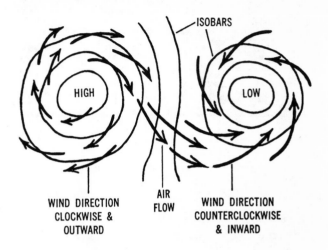

WIND DIRECTION CLOCKWISE & OUTWARD

AIR FLOW

WIND DIRECTION COUNTERCLOCKWISE & INWARD

When cool air is met and overrun by a warm air mass, a warm front is produced. The leading edge of the warm air mass, which is the front, slides up over the cool air and produces rain. On the other hand, when a cold air mass collides with and plows under warm air, a cold front is produced. The cold air flows low, under the warm air, because warm air rises and cold air sinks. With a cold front the warm air is pushed rapidly to

FIGURE 73: FRONTS

AN EXTRA-TROPICAL LOW WITH FRONTS SHOWN BY SYMBOLS

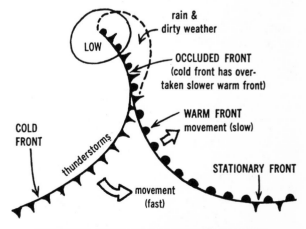

rain & dirty weather

OCCLUDED FRONT (cold front has overtaken slower warm front)

WARM FRONT movement (slow)

STATIONARY FRONT

COLD FRONT

thunderstorms

movement (fast)

COLD FRONTS OFTEN CLOSELY FOLLOW WARM FRONTS

FIGURE 74: CROSS SECTION OF A WARM AND COLD FRONT

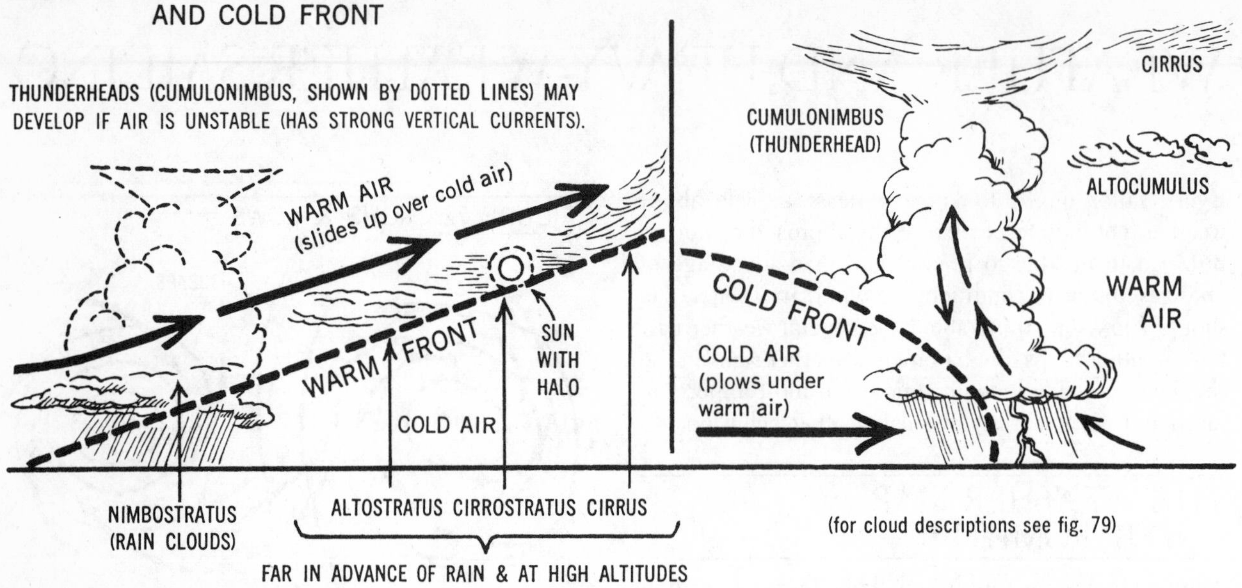

THUNDERHEADS (CUMULONIMBUS, SHOWN BY DOTTED LINES) MAY DEVELOP IF AIR IS UNSTABLE (HAS STRONG VERTICAL CURRENTS).

CIRRUS

CUMULONIMBUS (THUNDERHEAD)

ALTOCUMULUS

WARM AIR (slides up over cold air)

WARM AIR

COLD FRONT

WARM FRONT

SUN WITH HALO

COLD AIR

COLD AIR (plows under warm air)

NIMBOSTRATUS (RAIN CLOUDS)

ALTOSTRATUS CIRROSTRATUS CIRRUS

(for cloud descriptions see fig. 79)

FAR IN ADVANCE OF RAIN & AT HIGH ALTITUDES

---

high altitudes and violent thunderstorms can be formed (see Figure 74). When a cold and a warm front moving toward each other meet, stop, and interlock, we have a stationary front. When a fast-moving cold front overtakes a warm front which is moving in the same direction, the cool air in front of and the cold air behind the warm front meet to force the warm air upward. This is called a closed or occluded front, and it can have the characteristics of either a warm front or a cold front or both. Fronts are nearly always associated with some kind of weather disturbance.

The instrument for measuring atmospheric pressure is the *barometer*. This is a handy gadget which should be carried in the cabin of every cruising boat. Barometers measure air pressure in terms of the height of a column of mercury which the atmospheric weight will support (see Figure 75). A glass tube closed at the top but open at the bottom is filled with mercury. The bottom of the tube is placed in a dish filled with mercury. Atmospheric pressure pushing down on the mercury in the dish will support the column within the tube to approximately 30 inches in height under normal conditions. A high pressure pushing down on the mercury will push the column up high, but low pressure will cause the column to be low. Large ships often carry mercurial barometers which are based on the principle illustrated in Figure 75, but most small boats carry what are called aneroid barometers, based on a different principle, which are handier and less subject to damage.

In a very general sort of way, a high *glass* (high barometer reading) means good weather, while a low glass means bad weather. Unfortunately, however, it's not that simple. Other factors, such as the degree and rapidity of pressure change and the wind direction must be considered in making weather predictions. It is all-important to know not just what the pressure is when you read the barometer but to know what the trend is, whether the glass is rising or falling. This can be determined by noting the present reading (usually noted by manually setting a brass hand which lies overtop of the black pressure-indicating needle), then making a later reading to find the amount of rise or fall.

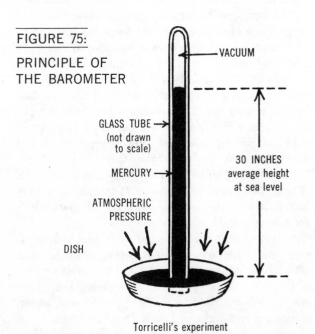

FIGURE 75:

PRINCIPLE OF THE BAROMETER

VACUUM

GLASS TUBE (not drawn to scale)

30 INCHES average height at sea level

MERCURY

ATMOSPHERIC PRESSURE

DISH

Torricelli's experiment

Here are some general rules to follow in making predictions from the barometer: When the barometer is falling and winds are from easterly quadrants, there is a good chance of foul, rainy weather. Generally, with winds *veering* (changing clockwise) to westerly quadrants, when the barometer is high and steady or slowly rising, the weather should be fair. For southerly winds, the barometer usually falls, but it rises for northerlies. A rising glass with a veering wind indicates fair weather, but a falling glass with a *backing* (changing counterclockwise) wind often means bad weather. A sudden rise in pressure indicates unsettled weather and often strong winds. An old nautical saying goes, "Quick rise after low portends a stronger blow." A gradual, steady fall indicates rainy and unsettled weather. A rapidly falling and extremely low glass indicates foul weather and perhaps severe storms.

LOCAL CONDITIONS

The actual wind in your area will depend not only on the general weather pattern but on particular local conditions and physical features. It is advisable for a sailor to keep records or mental notes of storms, areas of winds and calms, shifts of winds, where strong currents run, and so forth, because these conditions often repeat themselves. A skipper who can predict these things with reasonable accuracy can avoid unfavorable conditions and take advantage of those that are favorable.

An important part of any local weather picture is the morning and evening breezes—known respectively as *sea breeze* and *night wind*—caused by the unequal heating of the land and sea. Land heats more rapidly and cools more rapidly than water; therefore, the land is usually hotter than the water during the day, but cooler at night. When the hot air rises over the land, cool air from the sea flows in to fill the void, but at night the reverse is true; cool air over the land flows seaward to replace the relatively warmer air that has risen. At the times of day when the land and sea temperatures are about equal, usually some time between dusk and midnight or between dawn and mid-morning, the land-sea breezes cease to exist, sometimes causing a calm.

Irregular heating of air over land can greatly affect the velocity and direction of wind. Vertical currents rise over cities or towns, roads, and hot plains; but these currents fall over cool fields, woods, and inland bodies of water. This is one reason why breezes blowing from over the land, such as the east coast northwester, tend to be particularly gusty and shifty. A steady horizontal breeze is certain to be disrupted when it flows across strong vertical drafts of air.

Thermals, or hot-air updrafts, which occur along a shore when the land heats up, can benefit the sailor by producing a light wind fairly close to the shore. A breeze blowing across a shore can be beneficial by producing a favorable *slant*, a shifting that allows the boat to be lifted or pointed higher. Because of the earth's rotation, which produces the *coriolis effect* (a shifting to the right of wind in the northern hemisphere), and the fact that friction slows the wind's velocity over rough terrain, a land breeze tends to veer or shift clockwise after leaving a shore. An example of how the sailor might take advantage of this phenomenon is illustrated in Figure 76. Notice that the boat beating to windward along the shore is headed as it approaches the shore, but then she tacks when well into the land breeze, and on port tack she can sail parallel to the shore. When sailing near the land to get a favorable slant, however, one should not sail too close to high banks or high wooded areas. These shores can create a lee or wind shadow when the breeze is from off shore, and they can cause the wind to rebound and create turbulence when the breeze is blowing on shore (see Figure 77).

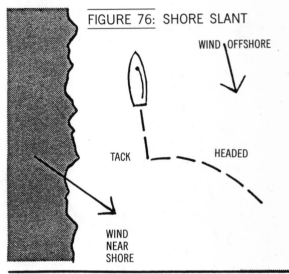

FIGURE 76: SHORE SLANT

WIND OFFSHORE

TACK   HEADED

WIND NEAR SHORE

FIGURE 77: WIND & HIGH SHORES

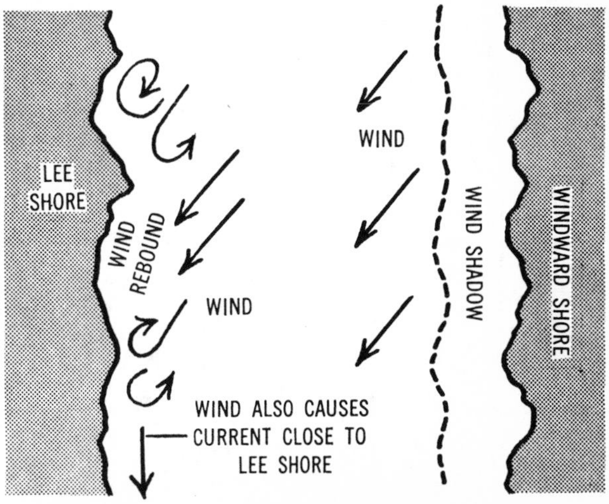

LEE SHORE

WIND REBOUND

WIND

WIND

WIND ALSO CAUSES CURRENT CLOSE TO LEE SHORE

WIND SHADOW

WINDWARD SHORE

Another factor that can cause irregularities in a breeze is variation in surface friction. Here again, physical features of the land play an important role. Tall trees, buildings, hedges, etc., will cause a lot of friction and thereby reduce the strength of a breeze. In fact, even small waves can reduce the wind's velocity near the water's surface. Winds are often lighter over a *tide rip*, where the water is roughened by the friction of tidal currents over a shoal or by two opposing currents.

TIDES AND CURRENTS

A good sailor is always aware of the current. He often calls it *tide*, but technically speaking, tide is the rise and fall of water which causes *currents*, the water's flow from one place to another. Tide is primarily governed by the gravitational attraction of the moon, but the sun

FIGURE 78: CURRENT

To determine current's direction, watch buoys and fixed objects in water such as fish stakes. Buoys usually lean in direction of flow. Current causes buoys and fixed objects to make rippled wakes.

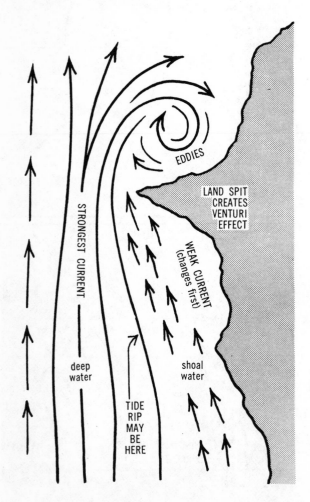

also exerts some influence. When the sun reinforces the moon's power of attraction (due to the earth, sun, and moon being in line), then the greatest range in tides occurs. These are called *spring tides*. But when the three heavenly bodies do not line up, the sun partially nullifies the moon's power of attraction and we have the smallest range in tides. These are called *neap tides*. Tides turn or change approximately every six hours and twelve minutes. Near these times, the tidal currents must stop to reverse direction of flow. Then we say that the water or tide is slack. Unusual conditions of wind and weather, however, can alter considerably the strength of a current and either speed up or delay its turning or changing direction.

Here is some general information concerning tidal currents: The shape of the shore line and the depth of the water have a great bearing on the strength and direction of a current. Where points of land stick out, the current flows fast and often swirls or forms back eddies behind the land (see Figure 78). Current flows with great strength and changes slowly in a deep channel or in the middle, deep part of a body of water. Conversely, current flows weakly and changes first near the shore in shallow waters. If you are sailing against the current, keep in shore where it is weak. If the current is with you, stay out in the middle, where the flow is strongest. If you are near shore and the current has just turned against you, consider going off shore, because the current might still be flowing the other way in open water. If you are sailing to windward against a foul or unfavorable current, try to arrange your course so that on one tack, the flow will push against your lee bow. A change in the current's direction, at the mouth of a river, for example, can be used to boost you to windward.

CLOUDS AND STORMS

Clouds are good indications of the weather, and they should be observed frequently when sailing. Figure 79 illustrates most of the cloud forms. High clouds are the *cirrus* and *cirrocumulus*. The former look like white, feathery wisps which sailors call *mares' tails*; while the latter are small white flakes or rippled, lumpy masses, which are known to sailors as a *mackerel sky*. Both these cloud forms can indicate wind. An old nautical adage goes, "Mackerel skies and mares' tails make lofty ships carry small sails." Generally, if these clouds are irregular and isolated, there is not much danger of bad weather, but if they are regular and thicken to fill the sky, bad weather might be expected. Another high cloud form, *cirrostratus*, gives a white hazy appearance and is responsible for the halo that sometimes encircles the sun or moon. This can be a bad-weather sign.

Clouds of medium heights are the *altocumulus* and

FIGURE 79: CLOUDS

CIRROCUMULUS "mackerel sky"
(over 20,000 ft.) can predict approach
of warm front in unstable air

ALTOSTRATUS (about 19,000 ft.) gray sheet
often warns of approaching warm front

CUMULONIMBUS "thunderhead" (thunderstorm
cloud)—can reach height of cirrus

CIRRUS "mares' tails" (over 25,000 ft.)
if thick often advanced forerunners
(24 hours or more) ahead of a front

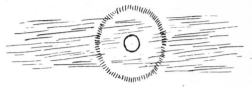

CIRROSTRATUS (over 20,000 ft.) whitish sheet
often causing halo around sun—can warn of
approaching warm front

ALTOCUMULUS (over 12,000 ft.) like sheep—
can warn of cold front in unstable air

STRATOCUMULUS (about 8,000 ft.) dark globular rolls

CUMULUS (over 4,000 ft.) fair
weather unless extreme towering up

NIMBOSTRATUS
(about 3,000 ft.)
dark rain cloud

STRATUS (about 1,500 ft.) gray sheet

the *altostratus*. The former is composed of small, lumpy white masses which resemble little rolls of wool and which, if very thick, often denote the approach of cold-front storms, while the latter is more like an amorphous, misty, gray sheet; it often precedes a warm front and can mean rain.

The low clouds are *stratocumulus*, *stratus*, and *nimbostratus*. The first is similar in appearance to altocumulus except the lower stratocumulus is gray, elongated, and often quite dark in spots. This is the highest of the low-cloud group. Stratus, the lowest cloud, forms a fog-like gray sheet which lies about fifteen hundred feet above the ground. Nimbostratus occurs when a stratus cloud puffs up to form a head. This is the true rain cloud. Ragged fragments of this cloud often break off and drift under the stratus layer. These are called *fractonimbus*, but sailors often call them *scud*.

The clouds with vertical development are called *cumulus* and *cumulonimbus*. These are generally low but can rise up to high altitudes. A cumulus is fairly flat on the bottom but has a puffy dome on top which looks like an irregular mound of cotton. Low cumulus are fair-weather clouds. However, cumulonimbus, often called the *thunderhead*, is a storm cloud. This is a lofty development of the cumulus which builds up to great heights, causing its top to flare out in the shape of an anvil. Its bottom is often dark and ragged. Cumulonimbus is the thunderstorm cloud which can have violent winds, rain, and even hail. Sailors are watchful for thunderheads.

Thunderstorms can result either from isolated masses of hot air rising rapidly into high cold air or from fronts. In the first case, storms usually arise in the afternoon of a hot summer day and occur in small, local areas. Cold-front storms (the second case) are the more violent, particularly in hot weather, and they are spread along the entire front.

When out sailing on a hot, summer afternoon, look for rising cumulus clouds on the horizon, generally somewhere to the west of you in the middle latitudes. Should they grow dark at the base and develop anvil tops, they have become thunderheads and you could well be in for a squall. In this case, if the storm is still some distance away on the horizon, head for the nearest harbor or an area where you may anchor. Quite often a calm precedes one of these storms, but not always. Play it safe; get your sails down, stop them well, and anchor in plenty of time. Thunderstorms are usually short-lived and are followed by fair weather.

Before leaving for a day's sail or a longer cruise, it is wise to check the weather bureau forecasts either in the paper or on the radio or television. Especially helpful are the NOAA VHF/FM broadcasts updated every two hours or so on such frequencies as 162.55, 162.40, and 162.475 MHz. Also check for storm warnings, displayed at some yacht clubs, weather stations, or boating centers. These warnings are shown in Figure 80.

Here are a few miscellaneous weather sayings which, most of the time, hold remarkably true:

"A red sky at night,
Is the sailor's delight,
But red sky in the morning,
Sailors take warning."

"Long foretold, long past;
Short warning, soon past."

"If the sun goes pale to bed,
'Twill rain tomorrow it is said."

"If the rain comes before the wind,
You'd better get your topsails in.
But if the wind comes before the rain,
Set them out again."

"When sound* travels far and wide,
A stormy day will like betide."

"Quick rise after low,
Portends a stronger blow."

SAILING IN A BLOW

Sailing a boat in heavy weather requires a special technique. The helmsman must take into consideration not only the force of wind on sails, but the force of seas as well. Failure to steer correctly in a seaway can result in heavy waves coming aboard, or the boat's being stopped dead and losing steerageway, or her broaching and being rolled over excessively. Foam and spray coming aboard merely cause a little discomfort, but a solid wave breaking on deck can cause real damage. When sailing to windward or close reaching across rough water, the helmsman should bear off enough to keep his boat moving in the *troughs* or valleys of the waves. When the boat begins to climb up a wave, he should luff to meet the wave nearly head on. If there is a particularly steep, curling *crest* or top that looks as if it might break aboard and the helmsman finds that he has not luffed sufficiently in advance so that the bow will meet it head on, then he should bear off slightly just before striking the wave top. This will lessen the impact. Luffing into a crest at the last minute will only cause the bow to slap into the sea and make it spill aboard.

*When sounds such as horns, bell buoys, etc., carry unusually well.

72

FIGURE 80: STORM WARNINGS

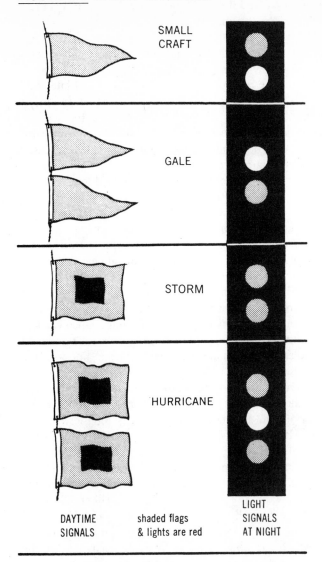

SMALL CRAFT		
GALE		
STORM		
HURRICANE		

DAYTIME SIGNALS   shaded flags & lights are red   LIGHT SIGNALS AT NIGHT

When sailing into head seas, a boat should not be sailed at excessive speeds because this will make her hit each wave with more force, but she should be kept moving. If the boat is stopped by a wave she might get in stays and not answer to her helm. Then she would be at the mercy of the next wave because the helmsman would be unable to luff into it. If the boat is slowed down a great deal by a sea, the helmsman should bear off to get his boat moving again.

When running before heavy seas, again, the boat should not be sailed at excessive speeds because this will either cause her stern to squat or be dragged down so that it encourages a *pooping sea* (one breaking over the stern), or else her bow could bury and cause her to broach to. Most authorities feel that even on this point of sailing, just enough speed should be maintained to make the boat responsive to her helm. When seas are high, the helmsman should keep the stern pointed directly at each wave. He may sail a little higher in the troughs, but he should bear off directly before it when near a crest. A sea rolling under the quarter can cause the boat to yaw and possibly broach to. In high winds on this point of sailing, it is often wise to lower the mainsail entirely and carry a *spitfire* (a small storm jib) sheeted in flat. This will help prevent yawing and help keep the boat stern to the waves.

REDUCING SAIL

If, when sailing in a strong breeze, you should find that your boat seems overburdened, is heeling excessively, and is burying her lee rail, then you must reduce sail. This can be done by removing sails or by reefing them. Whichever alternative is decided on, you must shorten sail so that a smaller but balanced sail plan remains. You will recall that this was mentioned in Section IV and illustrated in Figure 12. The important thing to remember is that sail should be reduced more or less equally on either side of the center of effort but with slightly more sail remaining forward to allow for the extra weather helm due to excessive heeling. For example, a yawl or ketch might sail with mainsail alone, jib and main, or just mizzen and jib, while a schooner might carry only her foresail or her jib and deeply reefed mainsail. A sloop can carry a jib and reefed main, while a cutter might carry a fore staysail alone. At any rate, the helm should be reasonably balanced.

There are two methods used to reef a sail: *roller reefing* and conventional reefing; the latter is done with lashings attached to the sail called *reef points*. At present, the most popular form of reducing a mainsail's area is with a simplified version of the points system called *jiffy reefing*, which will soon be described. With roller reefing the sail is merely rolled around its own luff or rolled up on its boom, which is turned round and round by a special crank near the gooseneck. Figure 81 shows two types of roller reefing. On small boats with roller reefing the boom is often turned by hand without using a crank handle. In order to let the boom turn, its sheet must be fastened by a swivel to the extreme after end of the boom or else the sheet must be secured by a claw ring, shown in Figure 81; otherwise the line would be rolled around the boom along with the sail. With roller reefing, the boom is usually turned after the sail is hoisted. The halyard should be eased off as the crank is turned, and the sail is wound around the boom. This is done until the sail area exposed to the wind has been reduced the desired amount. One person may have to pull the sail aft by its leech to make a smooth roll. On many sails, the lower batten is parallel to the boom so that it may be left in and rolled against the boom. But if this batten makes a right angle to the

FIGURE 81: ROLLER REEFING

A—WORM GEAR

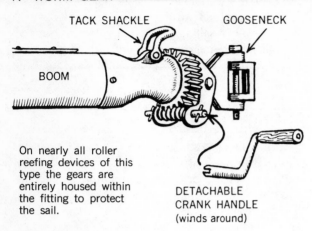

TACK SHACKLE   GOOSENECK

BOOM

On nearly all roller reefing devices of this type the gears are entirely housed within the fitting to protect the sail.

DETACHABLE CRANK HANDLE
(winds around)

B—RATCHET TYPE

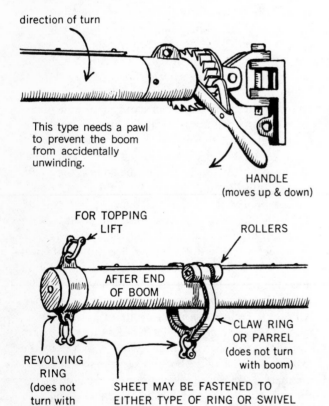

direction of turn

This type needs a pawl to prevent the boom from accidentally unwinding.

HANDLE
(moves up & down)

FOR TOPPING LIFT

ROLLERS

AFTER END OF BOOM

CLAW RING OR PARREL
(does not turn with boom)

REVOLVING RING
(does not turn with boom)

SHEET MAY BE FASTENED TO EITHER TYPE OF RING OR SWIVEL FITTING AT BOOM'S EXTREME END.

leech, it will not lie parallel to the boom; thus it should be removed from its pocket so that it will not be broken or bent if rolled around with the sail.

Conventional reefing requires a sail with reef points or a row of small eyelets through which a lashing may be passed (see Figure 82). Although experienced sailors often reef this kind of sail while it is hoisted, the beginner may find it easier to lower his sail when it is to be reefed by this method.

With conventional reefing, you should try to determine whether or not you will need to shorten down before leaving your harbor, because it is much easier to tie in the reef while at anchor. Should you later find you do not need the reef, it is easy to *shake out*, or untie, while you are sailing. Determining the need for reefing will depend not only on how hard it is blowing, but on what kind of a boat you have. A tender, easily heeled, narrow centerboarder with a large sail area and open cockpit should obviously be reefed long before a stiff keel boat with a self-bailing cockpit and a short rig. Generally speaking, however, you should reef when the wind grows fresh, when small trees begin to sway, and when a lot of waves have *white caps* or foamy tops. Remember this: weather will always appear more calm in a protected harbor than out in open waters.

Figure 82 shows a properly tied-in reef. The correct procedure is first to tie down the tack and then clew *cringles* with lanyards or short lashings called *earings*. Cringles are the two small *grommets*, or reinforced holes, at the luff and leech which are in line with the tops of the reef points. The tack cringle must be tied down around the boom directly below the cringle, but it also should be tied back to the after end of the boom or outhaul to prevent the sail from sliding forward.

Following this, the loose, excess foot of the sail is neatly rolled up to the boom and tied with the reef points. These are passed under the sail between the sail and the boom. Each reef point is tied to its opposite end, which is on the sail's other side. (Reef points run through small holes or eyelets in the sail.) The actual tying should be made with a reef knot (Figure 82) which has a bow so it can be easily released when the reef is shaken out. If the sail has more than one line of reef points, check to be sure that all the points tied are from the same row, otherwise the sail could be torn when it is hoisted. It is always preferable that the points be tied as illustrated in order that strain on the sail is more evenly distributed. But when the foot is attached to the boom with a bolt rope in a groove, requiring that lashings go around the boom, it is best not to use points but instead to use one long continuous lacing line which is wound spirally around the boom through the reef point eyelets.

The "jiffy" variation of conventional reefing is made possible by the shorter booms on modern boats and the great stability of the latest sail materials. This system speeds up the process by simplifying the clew earing, minimizing the need for points, and often securing the tack with a ring on a hook at the gooseneck as shown in Figure 82, *B*. Reefing can be done with minimal effort while the sail is hoisted. Customary steps are to set up

FIGURE 82: CONVENTIONAL AND JIFFY REEFING

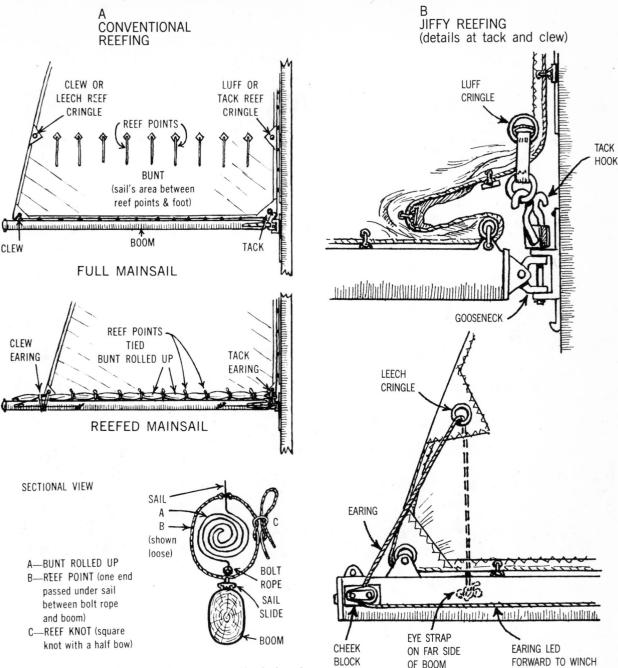

A CONVENTIONAL REEFING

CLEW OR LEECH REEF CRINGLE

REEF POINTS

LUFF OR TACK REEF CRINGLE

BUNT
(sail's area between reef points & foot)

CLEW

BOOM

TACK

FULL MAINSAIL

CLEW EARING

REEF POINTS TIED BUNT ROLLED UP

TACK EARING

REEFED MAINSAIL

SECTIONAL VIEW

A—BUNT ROLLED UP
B—REEF POINT (one end passed under sail between bolt rope and boom)
C—REEF KNOT (square knot with a half bow)

SAIL
A
B
(shown loose)
C
BOLT ROPE
SAIL SLIDE
BOOM

B JIFFY REEFING
(details at tack and clew)

LUFF CRINGLE

TACK HOOK

GOOSENECK

LEECH CRINGLE

EARING

CHEEK BLOCK

EYE STRAP ON FAR SIDE OF BOOM

EARING LED FORWARD TO WINCH

the topping lift, slack the mainsheet, ease the halyard until the tack grommet or ring can be put on the gooseneck hook, tension the luff, and then tighten the clew earing until the leech cringle is close to the boom. Clew earings are usually led as illustrated with the end of the line made fast around the boom or to an eye strap on one side directly under the grommet. Then the line is led up through the grommet, down to a cheek block at the boom's end, and thence forward to a winch either on the boom, deck, or mast. Finally, the loose bunt can be tied up with a few points or lacing line.

HEAVING TO

Sooner or later, every sailor will get caught out in a storm or a real blow. The beginner should be careful this does not happen to him before he has at least a little experience. When a skipper sees such weather developing, he must either make for a protected anchorage or prepare to stay out and take it. If he is far from a good anchorage and has sufficient *sea room* or distance off shore, it would probably be best for him to ride it out, particularly if the bad weather seems close.

In this case he should try *heaving to**, which means bringing the bow fairly close to the wind and stopping nearly all headway. Often, if the boat has an auxiliary, this can be done under the engine alone. The vessel should be given only enough forward speed to keep steerageway. A better but more troublesome method is heaving to under sail.

For this, it is best to have *storm sails*: a *storm trysail* and spitfire. These sails are shown in Figure 83. Both are small sails of heavy cloth. The trysail is loose-footed and usually does not attach to the boom. It can be bent to the mainmast with rope lashings as illustrated, but nowadays it is usually secured with slides on a track. The spitfire usually has a high-cut foot and its tack secured by a short pendant to keep it fairly far off the deck, away from solid spray. The trysail is customarily sheeted in flat on one side while the spitfire is sheeted to windward on the opposite side, and the helm is held or lashed down. (A tiller would be to leeward, on the same side as the trysail.) This is illustrated in

Figure 83. On a cutter or any boat with an inner forestay, the spitfire should be used as a storm staysail.

This is how a vessel should behave when so rigged: She will pick up a little headway in a puff and begin to head into the wind due to her helm being down. When she is fairly close to the wind, the trysail will luff and the jib will be aback. This will cause her bow to fall off, her trysail will fill, and she will repeat the process all over again. Her course is shown by the dotted lines in the diagram.

Of course, many boats not intended for extensive cruising will not have these storm sails. If this is the case, a small, heavy jib or staysail should be used for the spitfire, and a closed-reefed (reefed down to the highest series of reef points) or deeply rolled mainsail should be used instead of the trysail. Try to get far off the *lee shore** before beginning to set storm sails or even turning in a reef, because these operations can be painfully slow in rough weather.

---

*Strictly speaking, heaving to means lying near head-to-wind under counteracting sails, but J. C. Voss, the famous authority on small boat voyaging, used the term in a broader sense, to include other means of making a boat lie near head to wind.

*Lee shore—Some novice sailors are confused by this term. A lee shore is the shore which the wind is blowing *onto*. When the wind blows *from* a shore, a lee is provided by the land, but this is called a windward shore.

FIGURE 83: HEAVING TO (UNDER SAIL)

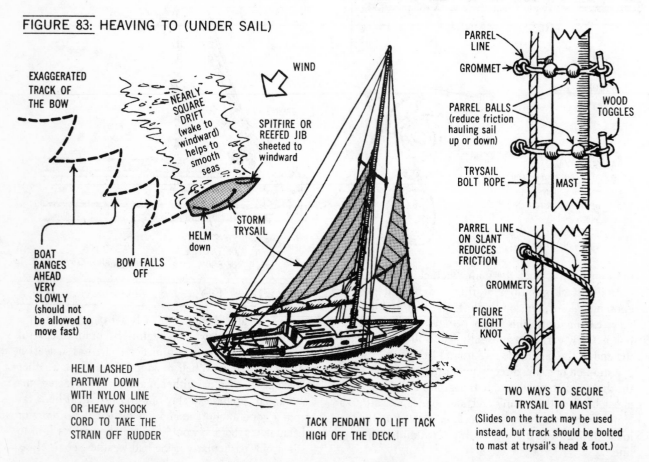

EXAGGERATED TRACK OF THE BOW

WIND

NEARLY SQUARE DRIFT (wake to windward) helps to smooth seas

SPITFIRE OR REEFED JIB sheeted to windward

STORM TRYSAIL

HELM down

BOAT RANGES AHEAD VERY SLOWLY (should not be allowed to move fast)

BOW FALLS OFF

HELM LASHED PARTWAY DOWN WITH NYLON LINE OR HEAVY SHOCK CORD TO TAKE THE STRAIN OFF RUDDER

TACK PENDANT TO LIFT TACK HIGH OFF THE DECK.

PARREL LINE

GROMMET

PARREL BALLS (reduce friction hauling sail up or down)

TRYSAIL BOLT ROPE

MAST

WOOD TOGGLES

PARREL LINE ON SLANT REDUCES FRICTION

GROMMETS

FIGURE EIGHT KNOT

TWO WAYS TO SECURE TRYSAIL TO MAST
(Slides on the track may be used instead, but track should be bolted to mast at trysail's head & foot.)

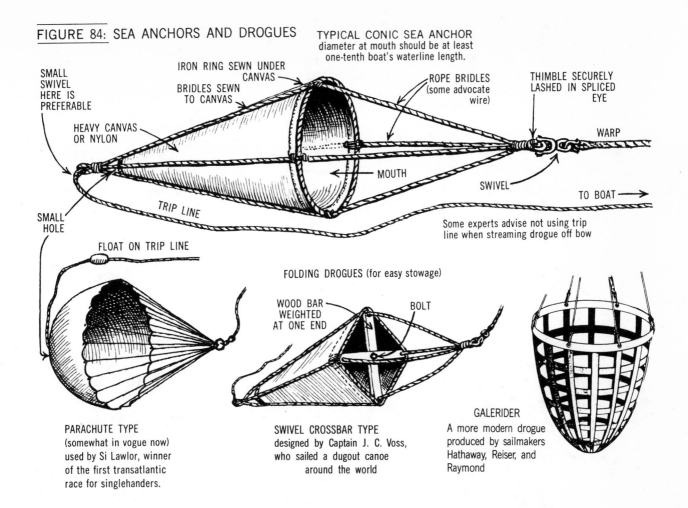

FIGURE 84: SEA ANCHORS AND DROGUES

TYPICAL CONIC SEA ANCHOR
diameter at mouth should be at least
one-tenth boat's waterline length.

SMALL SWIVEL HERE IS PREFERABLE

IRON RING SEWN UNDER CANVAS

BRIDLES SEWN TO CANVAS

HEAVY CANVAS OR NYLON

ROPE BRIDLES (some advocate wire)

THIMBLE SECURELY LASHED IN SPLICED EYE

WARP

MOUTH

SWIVEL

TO BOAT →

TRIP LINE

SMALL HOLE

Some experts advise not using trip line when streaming drogue off bow

FLOAT ON TRIP LINE

FOLDING DROGUES (for easy stowage)

WOOD BAR WEIGHTED AT ONE END

BOLT

PARACHUTE TYPE
(somewhat in vogue now)
used by Si Lawlor, winner
of the first transatlantic
race for singlehanders.

SWIVEL CROSSBAR TYPE
designed by Captain J. C. Voss,
who sailed a dugout canoe
around the world

GALERIDER
A more modern drogue
produced by sailmakers
Hathaway, Reiser, and
Raymond

Should the wind become so strong that even a deeply reefed main proves to be too much sail, you must lower it. In deep water offshore when the waves are not exceedingly steep and when the boat has ample reserve stability, a commonly used tactic is *lying ahull*, whereby all sails are lowered, hatches are *battened down* (closed and latched), and the helm is lashed down (rudder to windward). In steep waves, however, or when the boat is a centerboarder or other type with a low range of stability, this tactic might be too risky and the boat should probably be held end to the seas. One alternative is to run before the wind under bare poles (with no sail up) or with a storm jib sheeted flat. If the boat gets going too fast, drags such as lines, sails, or fenders might be towed astern. A better method of slowing speed, though, is to tow a *drogue* (a special device used to cause drag) such as those illustrated in Figure 84. Sea anchors, also illustrated, can reduce drift to a bare minimum when sufficiently large but may prevent the boat from yielding to the smash of seas. In smaller sizes, of course, they might be used effectively as drogues.

In former days, when the average cruising boat had a long keel and deep forefoot, sea anchors were frequently used from the bow to encourage a vessel to keep her head to the wind and waves. However, many modern boats of the type having a cut-away forefoot and a lot of windage forward will not readily lie to in this manner. A modern yawl or ketch might be able to lie to a sea anchor off the bow if a small sail is set and sheeted flat on the mizzen. Most boats of this type, however, will better hold their ends to the seas when anchors are deployed from the stern; but this tactic should only be used if the boat has plenty of freeboard aft and a self-bailing cockpit.

In the event that you find yourself close to or drifting in on a lee shore during a heavy blow, you must "claw off" or get distance off shore. This might be done with your auxiliary, if you have one, or with sail and engine, or with sail alone. Your sail plan for this action should be reduced but balanced with sails that will allow you to point or make distance to windward. If for some reason you cannot make distance off shore, drop your heaviest anchor if the depth of water allows. Then let out all the scope you have and, if you have an engine, run it slowly ahead to help the anchor hold your boat against the wind and sea. If your predicament is the result of having been caught in a sudden thunderstorm, take courage from the fact that these storms do not usually last long and you should be able to ride it out.

One last word on sailing in heavy winds: *Do not let your sails flap excessively.* Keep them filled as much as possible. Violent shaking and flogging in the wind is what usually causes a sail to blow out or rip. This is one reason why some skippers, when properly prepared and with their sails sufficiently shortened down, prefer to jibe in a blow instead of coming about so that the wind is continually filling the sails, not flapping them. Of course, jibing in a heavy blow should be done only when it is really necessary to change course, and the maneuver should be executed with great caution. Should you find it necessary either to tack or jibe, wait for a lull in the wind and also wait for a time when the water is relatively smooth. If you decide to tack instead of jibing, be sure you have plenty of way on so that you will not be stopped by a sea when head-topwind and be put in stays. This would cause you to lose maneuverability and your sails would whip and flap in the wind for an unnecessary length of time. Should this happen, back your jib immediately so that you will fall off on the other tack and get your sails filled again. The slight amount of luffing that sails do when a vessel is hove to will not hurt them seriously, but the violent whipping that occurs when the vessel is headed directly into the wind can be very harmful to them.

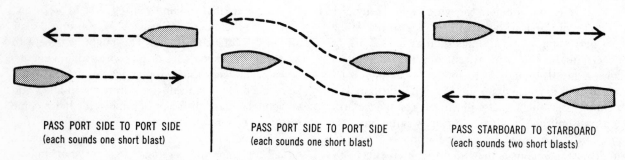

FIGURE 85: INLAND RULES (for motorboats or sailboats under power)

PASS PORT SIDE TO PORT SIDE
(each sounds one short blast)

PASS PORT SIDE TO PORT SIDE
(each sounds one short blast)

PASS STARBOARD TO STARBOARD
(each sounds two short blasts)

When vessels meet head on or nearly so, each vessel passes on the port side of the other unless the courses of such vessels are so far to starboard of each other as not to be considered meeting head and head.

RULES OF THE ROAD— NAVIGATION EQUIPMENT AND AIDS

RULES OF THE ROAD

With the waterways becoming more and more crowded, it is increasingly important for boat owners to become thoroughly familiar with boat traffic laws or *rules of the road*. These were formerly made complicated and confusing by differences in four sets of rules applying to waters within or adjacent to the United States, but in the early 1980s the various rules were brought into basic agreement. Rules governing U.S. waters were unified under the Inland Rules and these essentially agree, except in certain details, with International Rules which apply to vessels at sea. The beginning sailor should obtain and keep on hand a copy of the book *Navigation Rules, International-Inland* published by the U.S. Coast Guard.

Regardless of locality, there are separate rules for sailboats and motorboats. If you are moving under sail power alone, you are, of course, considered a sailboat; but should you be propelled by an auxiliary, you are considered a motorboat and so must be governed by motorboat rules. The rules are designed to cover every situation where vessels meet or cross, where there is any possibility of collision.

Figure 85 shows the Inland Rules for boats propelled by motor. You will notice in the diagrams that one vessel is often termed "give-way" while the other is termed "stand-on." This means that the former boat has to look out for the latter, which has the right of way. In one respect traffic rules for the water are similar to those for land in this country. Just as cars stay on the right-hand side of a road, boats keep to the right-hand side of a channel. The danger zone, shown in the diagram, extends from dead ahead to two points abaft the starboard beam. You must give way to any boat approaching you from any direction within that sector. If you are the stand-on boat, you must hold your course and speed. An overtaking boat is one which is overhauling another from astern or anywhere aft of two points abaft the beam.

Whistle signals shown in the diagram are for the purpose of reaching an understanding as to the method of passing. Three short blasts are given when your engine is in reverse. If there is confusion as to the other vessel's intention in a meeting or crossing situation, then five or more short, rapid blasts should be given and both vessels should stop or reverse until the misunderstanding is cleared up and proper passing signals are made.

Sound signals are also given in foggy weather. A sailing vessel underway shall sound her foghorn at intervals of not more than two minutes three blasts in succession, namely one prolonged followed by two short blasts. When at anchor in fog, a bell should be rung rapidly for about five seconds at intervals of not more than one minute. A power-driven vessel making way shall sound at intervals of not more than two minutes one prolonged blast. If this vessel is under way but not

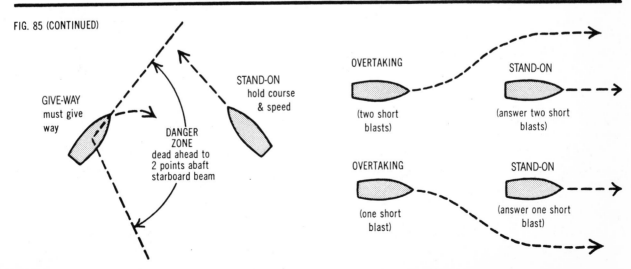

FIG. 85 (CONTINUED)

GIVE-WAY
must give
way

STAND-ON
hold course
& speed

DANGER
ZONE
dead ahead to
2 points abaft
starboard beam

OVERTAKING
(two short
blasts)

STAND-ON
(answer two short
blasts)

OVERTAKING
(one short
blast)

STAND-ON
(answer one short
blast)

FIGURE 86: RIGHT OF WAY SITUATIONS FOR BOATS UNDER SAIL— U.S. INLAND RULES

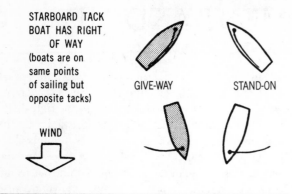

STARBOARD TACK BOAT HAS RIGHT OF WAY (boats are on same points of sailing but opposite tacks)

GIVE-WAY   STAND-ON

WIND

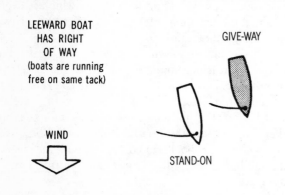

LEEWARD BOAT HAS RIGHT OF WAY (boats are running free on same tack)

GIVE-WAY

WIND

STAND-ON

OVERTAKING BOAT MUST KEEP CLEAR EVEN IF OVERTAKEN BOAT IS UNDER POWER

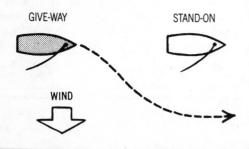

GIVE-WAY   STAND-ON

WIND

making way (progress) through the water, she shall sound at intervals of not more than two minutes two prolonged blasts in succession with an interval of about two seconds between them.

When a sailboat, under sail alone, converges with a motorboat, the former has the right of way except when the motorboat is being overtaken, in which case the sailboat must keep clear. Also sailboats must keep clear of vessels fishing with nets, lines, and trawls, but this rule does not apply to boats fishing with trolling lines or other gear that does not restrict maneuverability.

Figure 86 shows the rules that cover converging boats under sail alone, which are essentially the same for all waters. These rules state that when two sailing vessels are approaching one another so as to involve risk of collision, one of them shall keep out of the way of the other as follows:

(1) When each has the wind on a different side, the vessel which has the wind on the port side shall keep out of the way of the other.

(2) When both have the wind on the same side, the vessel which is to windward shall keep out of the way of the vessel which is to leeward.

(3) If a vessel with the wind on the port side sees a vessel to windward and cannot determine with certainty whether the other vessel has the wind on the port or on the starboard side, she shall keep out of the way of the other.

For the purposes of this rule the windward side shall be deemed to be the side opposite to that on which the mainsail is carried or, in the case of a square-rigged vessel, the side opposite to that on which the largest fore and aft sail is carried.

In a situation shown at the bottom of Figure 86, when one sailboat is overtaking another, the overtaking boat must keep clear, and this is even true if the stand-on boat is under power. In any converging situation the stand-on boat must hold a steady course until there is no longer risk of collision. Yacht-racing rules now generally agree with the rules of the road in that the starboard tack boat has the right of way over one on the port tack, and a windward boat must keep clear of one to leeward when both are on the same tack.

Rules of the road must be used with common sense and courtesy. There are times when sailboat skippers should not demand their right of way—for instance when they are converging with a large ship. As a matter of fact, the rules forbid a sailboat from hampering a large vessel in a narrow channel or one restricted in her ability to maneuver. Also, remember that many people who operate small motorboats and sailboats are not thoroughly familiar with the rules. Furthermore, some of the uninformed motorboat operators know very little about sailboats; so don't suddenly bear off or tack in front of a motorboat. Even if it seems obvious to you that you must do so, the motorboat skipper may not understand your maneuver; so, if possible, wait until he has passed before making the turn.

LIGHTS

When under way at night, between dusk and dawn, a vessel must display lights called *navigation* or *running lights* so that her presence and course will be known. These lights are colored white, red, or green and have several different arcs of visibility (see Figure 87). The

FIGURE 87: ARCS OF VISIBILITY FOR RUNNING LIGHTS

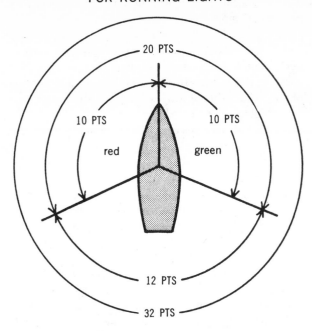

FIGURE 88: REQUIRED LIGHTS FOR MOTORBOATS & AUXILIARY SAILBOATS UNDER INTERNATIONAL RULES

required on the high seas and may be shown on U. S. waters

POWER OR POWER & SAIL
(20 meters [65.6 ft.] or less)

AUXILIARY (20 meters or less)
UNDER SAIL ALONE

ALSO FOR
SAILBOATS
(NO POWER)

WHITE LIGHT
FORWARD
OFF

12 PT. WHITE STERN LIGHT
VISIBLE 2 MILES
SEPARATE RED & GREEN
SIDE LIGHTS 10 PTS. EACH
VISIBLE 2 MILES*
20 PT. WHITE LIGHT FORWARD
VISIBLE 3 MILES†

12 PT. WHITE STERN LIGHT
VISIBLE 2 MILES
SEPARATE RED & GREEN
SIDE LIGHTS 10 PTS. EACH
VISIBLE 2 MILES

OR

OR

(STERN LIGHT
& WHITE LIGHT
FORWARD ARE
SAME AS ABOVE)

(STERN LT.
SAME AS
ABOVE)

WHITE LIGHT
FORWARD
OFF

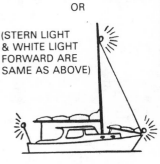

COMBINATION RED AND
GREEN BOW LIGHT, 20 PT.,
VIS. 2 MI.* MAY BE USED
IN LIEU OF SIDE LIGHTS

COMBINATION RED AND
GREEN BOW LIGHT, 20 PT.,
VIS. 2 MI.* MAY BE USED
IN LIEU OF SIDE LIGHTS

principal running lights which may be carried are: a separate starboard side light which is green with a 10-point visibility arc (as shown in the diagram); a separate port side light which is red and also covers 10 points; or a combination red and green bow light with each color covering 10 points; a white light on the mast facing forward and covering a 20-point sector; a white stern light covering 12 points; or a white stern light covering 32 points (all around the horizon).

While there are some lighting options under the rules, a sailboat* under 164 feet without an auxiliary which has separate red and green lights visible for two miles and a 12-point white stern light visible for two miles is properly equipped to sail on any waters.

Figure 88 shows the running lights required by the International Rules for auxiliary sailboats and motorboats, which *can* be used on inland waters and *must* be used on the high seas.

An *anchor light* or *riding light* is a 32-point white light displayed on the forward part of a vessel at anchor during the night. Although a vessel less than 23 feet long is not required to exhibit this light when not anchored near a narrow channel, fairway, or anchorage, it is obviously prudent to use the light anywhere there is boat traffic.

A SAILING VESSEL MAY ALSO SHOW OPTIONAL RED OVER GREEN 32 POINT LIGHTS WITH 2 MILE VISIBILITY AT OR NEAR THE TOP OF THE MAST.

A sailing vessel under 65.6 feet has the option of carrying the stern light and side lights combined in a single multisector light at the masthead. If this is done the above red over green optional lights may not be used.

A power-driven vessel less than 39.4 feet has the option of exhibiting a 32 point white light and side lights.

* 1 mile if vessel is under 12 meters (39.4 ft.)

† 2 miles if vessel is under 12 meters.

---

*Small sailing boats, under 23 feet, or row boats need only a flashlight or lantern to show on the approach of a vessel, but obviously they would be more safely equipped with proper running lights.

NAVIGATION EQUIPMENT

It is beyond the scope of this book to deal with the subject of navigation, but if the beginner intends to do any cruising at all, he should study all he can on the subject of *piloting* (close-to-shore navigation which makes use of soundings, sound signals, and visible landmarks). Whether cruising or not, every sailor should carry at least two indispensable pieces of navigation equipment: the *chart* (nautical map) and *compass*.

Charts give a wealth of information such as the depth of water, the location and description of channel markers and buoys, landmarks, the delineation of shoals with the description of the bottom, the location of obstructions, and much more. In addition, charts have what are almost essential to the navigator: *compass roses* (see Figure 89), which are graduated compass circles printed at various places on the chart. After drawing his course line on the chart, a navigator can draw a line exactly parallel to the course through a nearby compass rose to get his correct compass heading.

Boat compasses must be *gimballed* or mounted in such a way that they remain level with the horizon regardless of the motion or heeling of the boat. The compass should be located near the helmsman but away from iron objects or electrical equipment because these have a magnetic influence on the compass and

FIGURE 89: COMPASS ROSE

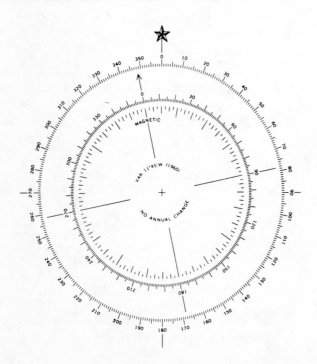

can ruin its accuracy. For greatest accuracy the compass should be *adjusted* (have its errors due to the boat's magnetic attraction reduced to a minimum) by a professional compass adjuster, but errors can be allowed for if the navigator makes up a *deviation card*. This is merely a card which records the *deviation* errors (errors due to shipboard magnetic influences) on various compass headings. The error for a certain heading can be obtained in a simple way by lining up from your boat two objects or landmarks shown on the chart. The chart gives their correct direction from you, and this can be compared with their direction shown on your compass.

The north point on a magnetic compass does not actually point to true north but generally toward *magnetic north*, an area located somewhat north of Hudson Bay. Directions on the chart, therefore, should be taken off the inner circle of the compass rose. This inner circle shows magnetic directions (not true directions) or how an adjusted compass (without deviation errors) actually points in the area covered by the chart.

Other basic piloting equipment not as essential as the chart and compass but extremely useful are (1) *parallel rules* for moving a course on the chart over to the nearest compass rose; (2) *dividers* for measuring distances on the chart; (3) *binoculars* for sighting distant buoys, channel markers, or other aids to navigation; (4) tide and current tables to predict times and heights of tides and strength and direction of currents in your area; (5) *Coast Pilots*, books which supplement information given on charts as to the description of ports, harbors, and coastlines; (6) *light and buoy lists* which also supplement the charts, giving detailed information on aids to navigation; (7) a *lead line*, a lead weight on the end of a marked line used to measure the depth of water, or an electronic depth sounder; (8) a small *radio direction finder*, a type of radio which can give radio bearings from standard broadcast stations or radio beacons. An R.D.F. can be a real blessing in foggy weather, and of course the radio can be useful in getting weather reports. This equipment can be obtained from any good marine supply dealer.

BUOYS AND CHANNEL MARKERS

As mentioned previously, buoys and other channel markers are shown on the chart. By consulting the chart, one can usually see instantly which way a channel runs and what shoals or obstructions to navigation the various buoys mark. This is one reason why it is important with a boat of almost any size to have on board charts to cover the water on which she sails.

Should you not have charts, however, the necessary information with regard to navigational hazards can be obtained by simply looking at a buoy or marker. This

FIGURE 90: U.S. BUOY SYSTEM
unlighted buoys without sound

NUN

CAN

RED BUOYS
even numbers

GREEN BUOYS
odd numbers

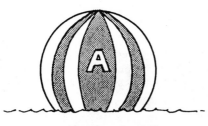

MID-CHANNEL BUOYS
red and white vertical stripes

preferred channel
lies to port (returning)

preferred channel
to starboard (returning)

NUN

CAN

JUNCTION OR OBSTRUCTION BUOYS
red and green horizontal bands

FIGURE 91: EXAMPLES OF SOUND & LIGHTED BUOYS

UNLIGHTED BELL

UNLIGHTED WHISTLE

newer types
have radar
reflectors

**LIGHTED BELL
BUOY**

**LIGHTED GONG
BUOY**

These buoys may be red, green, junction
or obstruction, or mid-channel

NOTE: In addition to the above federal markers there are
Intracoastal Waterway markers (along the Atlantic and Gulf
coasts) and state markers within certain state areas (such
as crowded inlets and lakes). However these marker sys-
tems are generally compatible.

Intracoastal Waterway aids to navigation are distin-
guished by a special yellow border or other yellow mark. On
this waterway, green markers are on the port and red markers on the starboard side of the channel entering from
north and east and traversed to south and west respectively.

State "Regulatory Markers" use international orange geometric shapes with a white background on a sign or buoy.
They are as follows:

UNIFORM STATE REGULATORY MARKERS

COLOR OF SHAPE—INTERNATIONAL ORANGE. BACK-
GROUND—WHITE. Diamond with cross means BOATS
KEEP OUT! Diamond shape warns of DANGER! Specific
danger (such as rock) is usually lettered inside the diamond. Circle marks CONTROLLED AREA such as a speed
limit (6 knots for example). Square or rectangle gives IN-
FORMATION such as the availability of gas.

information is given by a buoy's color, shape, or number. As you enter a U.S. channel from seaward the right-hand side is marked with red buoys and the left-hand side with green buoys. The classic means of remembering this is to think of the nautical "three R's," *Red, Right, Returning*. This means that when returning to a harbor (from seaward), you leave a red channel marker on your right or starboard side. Of course the opposite would be true when going out of a harbor: you would leave the red buoy to port.

Red buoys are marked with even numbers; green ones, with odd. Some red buoys have conical shapes and are called *nuns*. Green buoys are often cylindrical, and if so shaped are called *cans*. Buoys having red and white vertical stripes are *mid-channel markers*. They mark the middle of the channel; thus, boats should pass close by and to either side of these buoys. Buoys with red and green horizontal bands show the presence of either a *junction* in the channel, an *obstruction*, or a *middle ground*. These buoys should be given a wide berth or passed at some distance. They also may be passed on either side, but the color of the topmost band indicates the preferred channel. For example, if the band at the top is red, the preferred channel lies to port of the buoy when entering from seaward. Conversely, if the top band is green, the preferred channel lies to starboard when returning.

These buoys are illustrated in Figure 90, which shows the color green as black and red as gray (a shaded screen). Mid-channel buoys, formerly black and white, are now red and white, and they are spherical in shape or have a red spherical topmark. These buoys and obstruction (preferred channel) buoys are not numbered but they may be lettered.

Some especially important buoys are lighted or given sound or a combination of both. A few examples are illustrated in Figure 91. The addition of light or sound to a buoy merely makes it easier to identify. A light, sound, or combination light and sound buoy may be red, green, a mid-channel, or a junction or obstruction marker. Its meaning will depend primarily on the color of its paint and also on its number or letter if it has one.

Most navigation aids that are lighted show regular or irregular flashing lights. Lettered aids may even flash in Morse code. Green buoys show green lights; red buoys, red lights, mid-channels, white lights, and obstructions or junctions, red or green lights (depending on which side the preferred channel lies).

On the chart, a buoy is represented by an elongated diamond-shaped symbol with a dot at its end. This dot, which may have a magenta disc or radiating light rays to indicate lighting, marks the exact location of the buoy. The number of a buoy and its abbreviated description are next to its symbol. Some of the common, usual abbreviations are as follows: W—white, G—green, R—red, C—can, N—nun, S—spar, Fl—flash, F—fixed, and Occ—occulting, which is a steady light totally eclipsed at intervals. For a thorough understanding of buoys and their lights or other aids to navigation, the beginning sailor should study the charts, Light Lists, and Coast Pilots.

SAFETY AND EMERGENCIES

Every sailor, whether a beginner or not, should be aware of safety every minute he is afloat. This does not mean that he should be a timid skipper or a worrier who is overly cautious and lets this interfere with his fun. It simply means that he should carry the proper safety equipment and that he should plan ahead how to cope with any possible emergency.

SAFETY EQUIPMENT

There are special, legal, safety-related requirements for motorboats and auxiliaries (including those with outboard motors) under 65 feet long. These requirements include: back-fire flame arresters for carburetors, ventilation for engine compartments, sound signalling devices (whistle and bell for vessels 39.4 feet or longer), fire extinguishers, PFDs (personal flotation devices), visual distress signals (flares, smoke bombs, distress lights, etc.), and navigation lights (discussed in the previous section). Exact minimum requirements may be obtained from the Coast Guard, but it should be kept in mind that minimum equipment lists contain legal requirements only and not all the equipment that a boat ought to carry. How much and what kind of equipment you carry will, of course, depend on the size and kind of boat as well as for what purpose and in what area she will be used.

Important equipment for a small, open sailboat would include the following: Coast Guard approved PFDs, at least one for each person on board (there should be additional buoyant cushions); at least one adequately heavy anchor with ample anchor line; a pump and bailer or bucket for bailing out the bilge in the event the boat should leak, ship water, or capsize; and a paddle. If she is larger than a dinghy, the boat should carry tools (at least a knife, screwdriver, and pliers); spare parts (screws, bolts, shackles, extra blocks, etc.); a sewing kit with needles, a *palm* for pushing the needle, thread, beeswax, and a ball of *marline* or strong twine; a horn or whistle; a first-aid kit; docking lines; a chart of the local area; and a small compass. In addition, at night, of course, she must be equipped with navigation lights (described in the previous section) and should have a flashlight. If the boat has an auxiliary, she must have the flame arresters, ventilators, and fire extinguishers previously mentioned. Additional equipment, unessential but certainly desirable, would be: a

sponge for obtaining a completely dry bilge, a canvas cockpit cover, a boat hook, fenders, spare lines, sail or waterproof adhesive tape, and lubricating oil.

A larger, cruising sailboat with cabin should have all of this equipment plus distress signals (flares); a bell for ringing when at anchor in fog; a barometer; additional tools (including an assortment of wrenches, a hatchet, hacksaw, and hammer); tapered wooden plugs that may be driven into a round hole in the event of the failure or breaking of a through-hull fitting; drinking water and food; a kerosene lantern; storm sails or at least an extra working sail; matches stored in a watertight container; spares (flashlight batteries, hardware, and engine parts if there is an engine); at least one ring buoy—a doughnut-shaped life preserver, preferably the horseshoe type illustrated in Figure 92, hung near the cockpit where it can be instantly thrown overboard; a water light or floating light (illustrated in Figure 92), which may be thrown in the water if someone falls overboard at night; at least one extra anchor with line; a small tackle; and possibly a sea anchor or drogue.

FIGURE 92: LIFESAVING DEVICES

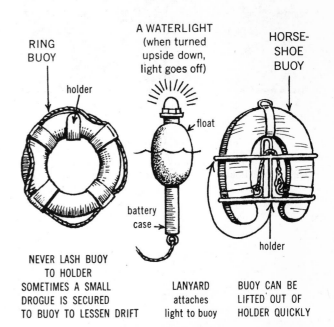

RING BUOY

holder

A WATERLIGHT
(when turned upside down, light goes off)

float

battery case

HORSE-SHOE BUOY

holder

NEVER LASH BUOY TO HOLDER
SOMETIMES A SMALL DROGUE IS SECURED TO BUOY TO LESSEN DRIFT

LANYARD attaches light to buoy

BUOY CAN BE LIFTED OUT OF HOLDER QUICKLY

NOTE: handy device is inflatable pocket life preserver pack.

FIGURE 93: RIGHTING AFTER CAPSIZING

If float (life preserver for example) is fastened to masthead to prevent boat from turning upside down, secure float to halyard so that it can be pulled down after boat is righted.

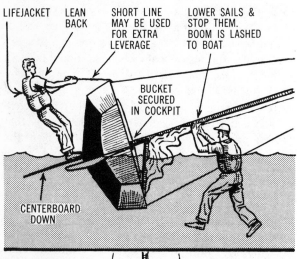

LIFEJACKET — LEAN BACK — SHORT LINE MAY BE USED FOR EXTRA LEVERAGE — LOWER SAILS & STOP THEM. BOOM IS LASHED TO BOAT — BUCKET SECURED IN COCKPIT — CENTERBOARD DOWN

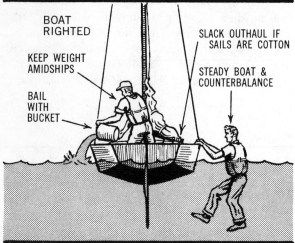

BOAT RIGHTED — KEEP WEIGHT AMIDSHIPS — BAIL WITH BUCKET — SLACK OUTHAUL IF SAILS ARE COTTON — STEADY BOAT & COUNTERBALANCE

IF RESCUE CRAFT IS PRESENT:

Rescue craft should stand by some distance away from capsized sailboat until after righting. From rescue craft, bow of righted (but still swamped) sailboat can be lifted to let water in cockpit flow out over stern. Towing swamped boat slowly for short distance will also cause water to flow out over the stern. After water has been removed as much as possible by towing or lifting bow, towing should be stopped, and bailing should begin with bucket or pump. Some small racing boats have transom bailers (openings with hinged flaps in transoms) which aid in water removal when boat is towed or sailed. Boat's forward movement causes water to rush aft through opening. Never tow a boat unless she is righted. Tow lines should be made fast around mast.

CAPSIZING

The two most probable emergencies the sailor will face, whether he is a beginner or not, are capsizing and running aground. Neither of these need be serious if proper action is followed.

Boats which are most susceptible to capsizing are small centerboarders with open cockpits. It is extremely rare for boats having ballasted keels to upset. The two most common causes of capsizing are an accidental jibe and carrying too much sail in a strong or puffy breeze. Jibing accidentally is often caused by sailing excessively by the lee or by inattentiveness of the helmsman (see Section VIII). Capsizing in a strong breeze is often a result of not shortening sail soon enough or of the lack of alertness in watching for and anticipating puffs. Expert racing skippers frequently capsize, however, because they sometimes prefer to carry all possible sail in a breeze, especially downwind, even at the risk of upsetting. It should make the beginner feel a little better about capsizing to realize that even the best sailors do it occasionally.

Let us briefly review some basic principles already mentioned which help to avoid capsizing: When running in a strong wind, do not sail by the lee (keep the wind more on your quarter); wait for a lull in the wind before jibing and pull your main sheet in carefully, so that it will not become fouled when it is slacked off after the boom crosses over; shift your weight to windward as soon as the boom swings across; don't round up into the wind too sharply or suddenly after jibing as this can cause additional heeling; if you are not properly shortened down for the breeze, consider coming about instead of jibing; watch closely for puffs striking the water, and when reaching or beating, be ready to luff as you meet them; when your boat heels too far (generally when she dips her rail), luff, slack sheets, and hike to windward; remember not to cleat the main sheet; be prepared for a hard puff when sailing out from under a lee; and finally, keep way on your boat for maneuverability so that you may luff up instantly.

Let us suppose, however, that you have not been quite cautious enough, and that you find yourself heeled to the point of no return. In other words, you are capsizing. The sheets are slack and the helm is alee but still you are turning over. At this time, you and your crew should be scrambling for the high side if you are not already there. Should you be quick enough, you might possibly be able to hang over the side, stand on the centerboard, and right the boat. At any rate, no one in the boat should be on her leeward side at this time because if this happens, not only will the boat's stability be lessened, but the person might become caught or entangled under the sails.

Now you are capsized. Your boat is lying on her side

with her mast and sails in the water. Have one of your crew stand on the lowered centerboard where it protrudes through the bottom if the mast's head begins to sink. Some boats with a lot of flotation are *self-rescuing*, meaning that they can be righted immediately without shipping much water. If your boat cannot be righted at once, however, see that all your crew are present and safe, then pull your life preservers out of the cockpit and have each person put one on if the preservers are the vest type. If any member of your crew is a nonswimmer, he should have had one on before you got under way. If the masthead still tends to sink (this will be unlikely with your crew on the centerboard), fasten a life preserver to the masthead. The cardinal rule for conduct after capsizing is, *stay with the boat*. Almost every boat, regardless of her construction and material from which she is built, is designed to float if she is capsizable. If you stay with your boat, she will help support you, and you can also be more easily spotted by rescuers.

At this point many articles such as paddles, cushions, bailers, etc., will begin to float out of the cockpit; so you should quickly retrieve and lash them to the boat. Then you should make plans for trying to right your boat in order to bail her out.

The proper procedure for righting a capsized boat is illustrated in Figure 93. First, try to anchor or at least turn your boat so that her bow is held into the wind. Then you may have to get your sails down and loosely furled. Have your crew, who are standing on the centerboard, lean backwards while holding onto the rail. Your boat should slowly right herself. You or another crew member should be on the boat's low side to act as a counterbalance to prevent her from capsizing the opposite way.

After this, try to bail her out with a bucket or bailer. If your boat has sufficient flotation, you can climb aboard in order to pump or bail much more effectively. Climbing aboard will be difficult without recapsizing the boat. Climb over one side of the stern as a crew member puts some of his weight on the other side to keep the boat balanced. Then once you are aboard, keep your weight amidships.

With a little luck, small seas, and the proper flotation you can empty your boat, hoist your sails, and be on your way as though nothing had happened. Should your flotation, the seas, and luck be against you, simply hail a passing boat and wait for rescue. But beware of a rescue craft getting your lines fouled in her propeller, and beware of her bumping into your boat. Never let your boat be towed while capsized. She should only be towed upright, at low speeds, and preferably when she has been bailed out.

With many small boardboats (p. 14) having ample flotation, sail need not be lowered. Normally it is only necessary to stand on the daggerboard to right the boat.

As mentioned in Section XI, before purchasing a boat that may be capsized, you should check its flotation. Many wooden centerboarders have sufficient buoyancy, but boats of fiberglass, metal, or wood boats with ballasted keels or heavy engines nearly always need added buoyancy. This may be in the form of air tanks, watertight compartments, air bags, or an aerated, expanded material such as styrofoam or polyurethane. Flotation should be placed so that a boat will float fairly level when swamped (not down by the bow or stern). A boat should float high enough when swamped so that the top of her centerboard well is above the water; otherwise, as the boat is bailed out, water will flow in through the well (see Figure 94). The lower the flotation is placed in a boat, the higher she will float (Figure 94).

FIGURE 94: FLOTATION

It is preferable that there be sufficient flotation to keep top of centerboard well above water when two people are in cockpit of swamped boat.

LOW CENTERBOARD WELL (water flows in)

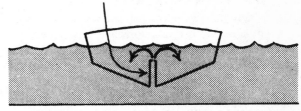

If opening at top of well is partially closed and well is below water, well opening might be partially sealed by stuffing it with rags.

HIGH FLOTATION

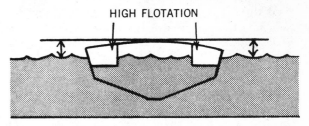

Low flotation is best, but it will increase boat's tendency to turn turtle (upside down) when capsized.

LOW FLOTATION

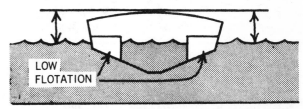

The best type of flotation is probably built-in, watertight air tanks filled with aerated, expanded material such as styrofoam or polyurethane (in case of leak or puncture in tank).

GROUNDING

More common than capsizing, perhaps, is grounding or running aground. No beginner should feel ashamed when this happens, because it can happen to the best of sailors. The most usual reasons for running aground are failure to read the chart or failure to observe buoys. Particular care should be taken to avoid grounding on a rocky bottom and to avoid a hard grounding, at fast speed, on any type of bottom. A gentle grounding on a soft bottom will not hurt a boat which is properly built.

It is usually easy to get off a shoal with a centerboarder. The board is simply pulled up. However, care should be taken to see that the boat is not blown further on shore as the centerboard is raised. This might be accomplished by merely poling off with a spinnaker pole, boat hook, or paddle in a small boat. Larger boats might have to be turned so that they are headed away from the shoal, or their auxiliary or anchor might have to be used if they are being blown in on a lee shore.

Freeing a keel boat is much more difficult. If the boat is hard aground, you may be released simply by waiting for high tide—unless you happened to run aground when the tide was highest.

After running aground, you should lower sail to keep from being blown further ashore, and then survey the situation. Look at the buoys and the chart to find out where the deep water is. If you have not run aground very hard, you may be able to back off under your engine, if you have one. Otherwise, you might be able to kedge off, by putting out an anchor and pulling on the anchor line. The anchor may be carried off from the boat in a dinghy, or by wading in the water, or it might be thrown out, though it is doubtful that you could throw any anchor other than a light one far enough for it to be effective. If you know exactly where the deep water is, and this could be determined by sounding, you might turn your boat toward the deep water, hoist and sheet in your sails in an attempt to heel the boat down so that she will draw less water, and then kedge from the bow so that your boat is pulled forward. This should be done only if the vessel is grounded on a soft bottom, because if her keel is embedded in a hard bottom it could be twisted or gouged when the boat is turned. This is not likely, but it has happened.

Learn the underwater shape of your boat so you know where she is deepest. Sometimes a keel can be lifted off the bottom by putting all the crew forward so that the stern rises, or this might be done while the boat is heeled over. Extra pulling power can be obtained from the kedge by using a tackle or by putting the anchor line around a winch.

If all these suggestions fail to free your vessel, you will probably have to get a motorboat to pull you off at high tide. Care should be taken when making fast the tow line. Don't put it around any cleat which is not solidly through-bolted; otherwise, it might pull off. It is often a good idea to make the tow line fast around the base of the mast at the partners.

MAN OVERBOARD

Another emergency to which you should give prior thought is the possibility of losing a crew member overboard. Life preservers should be carried in or within easy reach of the cockpit. These should be ring buoys or horseshoe buoys on large boats but could be floating cushions on small boats. In the event that a crew member falls overboard while you are under way, your first reaction must be to throw him a preserver. Don't throw it directly at him, particularly when using a heavy ring buoy, because you might hit him in the head! Keep your eyes on the man overboard every second; and if you are under motor power, swing the stern away from him so that he will not be cut by the propeller.

If under sail, the best procedure for returning to the overboard victim is either a quick jibe or the maneuver referred to by the U.S. Naval Academy as the "quickstop," whereby the boat is immediately luffed into the wind, tacked, and hove to with her jib aback. Both these methods will keep the boat close to the victim and keep him in sight. Jibing is often the quicker method but cannot be done immediately when certain gear such as an offcenter boom vang or mizzen staysail is carried. After a boat is quick-stopped she is borne off, the jib is lowered, and she is headed downwind under her sheeted-in mainsail. When slightly downwind of the victim, the boat is jibed and headed just to windward of him. The mainsail can be backed to kill headway. Whether jibing or quick-stopping it is usually better to pick up the victim on the lee side because it is lower and provides more protection. A line should be thrown to the victim when approaching him, and he should be lashed alongside until aids for recovery can be rigged. These aids might be a ladder, looped lines, or a tackle rigged from the mainboom or a halyard.

A shorthanded method of recovery, currently in vogue, is that which uses a *Lifesling*. Developed by the Sailing Foundation of Seattle, Washington, the Lifesling is a buoyant, flexible horsecollar attached to the boat with a long floating line. When a person is seen falling overboard, the Lifesling is thrown in the water and the boat is quick-stopped. Then she circles around the victim towing the Lifesling astern until he can grab the line and get into the sling. After this, the victim is hauled to the boat, secured alongside, and lifted aboard with a tackle. Figure 95 shows how the boat quick-stops and then circles the victim. Sold at most chandleries,

1 Shout "man overboard!" to your crew.

2 Throw life buoy.

3 Have a crew member keep eyes on victim.

4 Jibe or quick stop in most cases.

THE QUICK JIBE

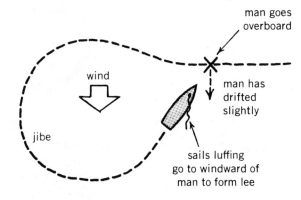

Hang looped or knotted lines or ladder over lee side to assist man getting aboard.

THE QUICK-STOP AND LIFESLING DEPLOYMENT

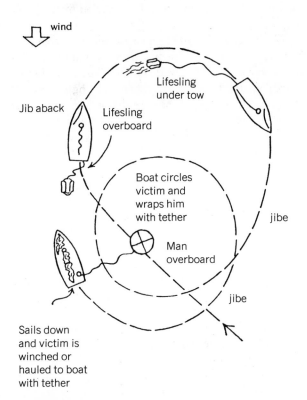

Lifeslings are packaged in yellow cloth pouches (marked with instructions) that can be secured to a stern pulpit.

It is a good idea to practice rescue operations occasionally. Throw overboard a life preserver or some other floating object and practice quick-stopping and jibing around to pick it up. A good rule to remember is never to lash the ring or horseshoe buoy to your boat. You would waste precious time cutting it loose. Secure the buoy so that it merely rests on a hook and may be lifted off and thrown at a moment's notice.

MISCELLANEOUS SAFETY MEASURES

(1) Carry all the equipment described as important in the first part of this section.

(2) When on any boat, wear topsiders or deck shoes, shoes with soles designed to afford maximum traction on slippery decks. Avoid, or at least be careful when stepping on varnished surfaces wet with spray or rain. These are extremely slippery.

(3) Learn to swim well. If taking out a nonswimmer for a sail, see that he wears a life jacket from the time he comes aboard. Learn how to perform artificial respiration. The method generally thought to be most effective is mouth-to-mouth resuscitation.

(4) Familiarize yourself with distress signals. They are: repeated raising and lowering of arms outstretched to each side for small boats; continuous sounding of a whistle, horn or bells; SOS (··· ––– ··· for a Morse code SOS signal); a gun fired at one-minute intervals; red flares or parachute flares showing red lights; flames on the vessel, from burning oil in a pan, for example; international code flags N C; a square flag with a ball above or below it; rockets or shells, bursting in the air with a loud report and throwing red stars, fired one at a time at short intervals; alarm signals from radio, radiotelegraph, radiotelephone, or EPIRBs (emergency position-indicating radio beacons); a flashing strobe light; the spoken word "Mayday" over the radiophone; an orange smoke signal; and hoisting the ensign, the yacht national flag or the U.S. flag, upside down.

(5) Always carry a knife with you. You never know when you might have to cut a line in an emergency.

(6) If your boat has an auxiliary, be very cautious when fueling. Do not spill fuel or overflow the tank. Keep nozzle of gas hose in contact with fill pipe leading to tank. This is to prevent a possible spark from static electricity. Extinguish fires and lights and cease smoking before fueling. After fueling, air out your boat thoroughly for at least five minutes and do not start the motor if you smell gas fumes in the bilge. If your tanks are aft, gas up with the bow headed into the wind to

prevent fumes from being blown down the companionway into the cabin.

(7) See that your gas tanks are properly installed with fill pipes firmly attached to deck plates. The fill pipe needs a flexible section to avoid fatigue from vibration, and the entire system should be electrically grounded. Vent pipes must lead to the open air, away from any hull opening. They should be bent down and/or in a full circle to prevent entry of rainwater or spray. Figure 96 shows correct and incorrect, dangerous installations.

(8) Keep your bilges clean, free of oil and gas. Carry at least the minimum equipment required by the Coast Guard. Although vessels built before July 31, 1980, are not required to have powered ventilation, it is important for maximum safety that every boat with an enclosed gasoline engine and starting motor has an effective blower.

FIGURE 96: GAS TANK INSTALLATION

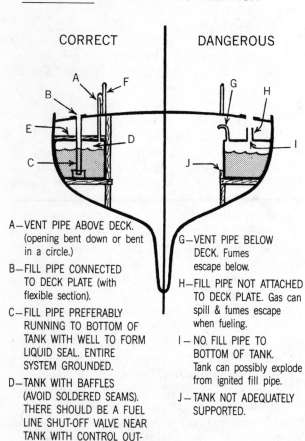

CORRECT   DANGEROUS

A—VENT PIPE ABOVE DECK. (opening bent down or bent in a circle.)

B—FILL PIPE CONNECTED TO DECK PLATE (with flexible section).

C—FILL PIPE PREFERABLY RUNNING TO BOTTOM OF TANK WITH WELL TO FORM LIQUID SEAL. ENTIRE SYSTEM GROUNDED.

D—TANK WITH BAFFLES (AVOID SOLDERED SEAMS). THERE SHOULD BE A FUEL LINE SHUT-OFF VALVE NEAR TANK WITH CONTROL OUTSIDE TANK'S COMPARTMENT.

E—PADDED SUPPORTS OR STRAPS AT TOP AS WELL AS SIDES AND BOTTOM OF TANK.

F—VENT SECURELY FASTENED TO COAMING, CABIN SIDE, OR INSIDE WINCH BASE.

G—VENT PIPE BELOW DECK. Fumes escape below.

H—FILL PIPE NOT ATTACHED TO DECK PLATE. Gas can spill & fumes escape when fueling.

I—NO. FILL PIPE TO BOTTOM OF TANK. Tank can possibly explode from ignited fill pipe.

J—TANK NOT ADEQUATELY SUPPORTED.

NOTE: Storage battery should be in ventilated lead-lined or fiberglass box with a cover to prevent metal objects from falling on battery terminals

(9) When in rough weather, heed this old nautical saying, "One hand for the ship and one hand for yourself."

(10) Do not stand with your foot in a coil of line, and do not stand in the angle by a block or light fitting, in case the block or fitting should fail. This is explained in Figure 97.

FIGURE 97:
ROPE SAFETY

DON'T STAND WITHIN ANGLE

50 lbs.

50 lbs.

100 lbs. strain at block & fitting

LINE HELD TOO CLOSE TO BLOCK

NOTE: Stand clear of a nylon line under great strain. If it breaks its elasticity can cause a dangerous whiplash.

(11) When pulling on a line which runs through a block, do not grab the line close to the block. Should the line start to run toward the block, you might lose a finger (see Figure 97).

(12) Be cautious when slacking off wire sheets or halyards on winches. Be sure you thoroughly understand how the winches work. Get an experienced sailor to explain their operation. When hoisting sail with a screw-toggle reel winch be sure the brake is on. Lower sail with the handle removed. Do not stand with your head near a winch handle while the winch is being cranked in. The handle could slip out of the hand of the winch operator and hit you in the head.

(13) Get in the habit of checking fittings to see that they are sound and are not pulling loose, and particularly check nuts on stays and turnbuckles. It is far safer to use cotter pins (wrapped in tape) instead of lock nuts on turnbuckles.

(14) If you have an auxiliary and tow a dinghy, watch for the dinghy's painter or tow line getting fouled around your propeller. This is particularly apt to happen when you have your engine in reverse. A fouled propeller can sometimes be cleared by cautiously reversing the engine momentarily if fouled when going ahead or by going ahead if fouled while in reverse.

(15) If you are in a small boat, be especially careful about overloading. People are often tempted to overload a small dinghy. Also, do not stand up in a small

dinghy or step on her side. You are almost asking to capsize.

(16) Use utmost care when going aloft in a *bosun's chair*, a small wooden seat on which a person sits so that he may be pulled up the mast with a halyard. If possible, this should only be done while at anchor or at dock in calm waters. The person being pulled aloft should hold on firmly to the mast or rigging until he is where he wants to be—at which time the halyard is securely cleated and hitched on its cleat. No one should stand under the man working aloft—he may drop a tool. The lowering operation should be done slowly and gently with a turn around the winch or cleat.

(17) See that your decks are clear of nonessential fittings which may trip passengers or crew, and if your boat has a cabin house, see that there are hand rails on its top to hold onto in rough weather. Be sure there are plenty of through-bolted grab rails below.

(18) Keep a lookout at all times.

With the conclusion of this section on safety, the essentials of sailing have been covered. The time has come to go sailing. Books alone cannot make a sailor of a landsman. Theory must be put to practice. I wish the reader fair sailing with moderate winds and bright waters ahead!

INDEX

4183